A Guide
to the
Overmountain Victory
National Historic Trail

Other titles by Randell Jones

Before They Were Heroes at King's Mountain, 2011
      Daniel Boone Footsteps, publisher
          Full Edition
          Virginia Edition
          North Carolina/Tennessee Edition
          South Carolina/Georgia Edition

In the Footsteps of Daniel Boone, 2005, John F. Blair, Publisher
      Willie Parker Peace History Book Award, 2006
      North Carolina Society of Historians

On the Trail of Daniel Boone, 2005, companion DVD
      Daniel Boone Footsteps, publisher
      Paul Green Multimedia Award, 2006
      North Carolina Society of Historians

In the Footsteps of Davy Crockett, 2006, John F. Blair, Publisher

Scoundrels, Rogues, and Heroes of the Old North State
      by Dr. H.G. Jones, co-editors: Randell and Caitlin Jones
      2004/2007, The History Press, Charleston, SC

All available through Daniel Boone Footsteps
      www.danielboonefootsteps.com
      1959 N. Peace Haven Rd., #105
      Winston-Salem, NC 27106
      DBooneFootsteps@gmail.com

A Guide to the Overmountain Victory National Historic Trail

by Randell Jones

author of

Before They Were Heroes at King's Mountain

Daniel Boone Footsteps
Winston-Salem, North Carolina

The maps presented in this book were created by the
National Park Service. They are in the public domain
and used here in accordance with policies published at
www.nps.gov/carto. All map segments are shown at a
consistent scale. None have been altered for any content.

For all those who have walked
in the footsteps of
America's overmountain and backcountry
Patriot militia

A GUIDE TO THE OVERMOUNTAIN VICTORY NATIONAL HISTORIC TRAIL

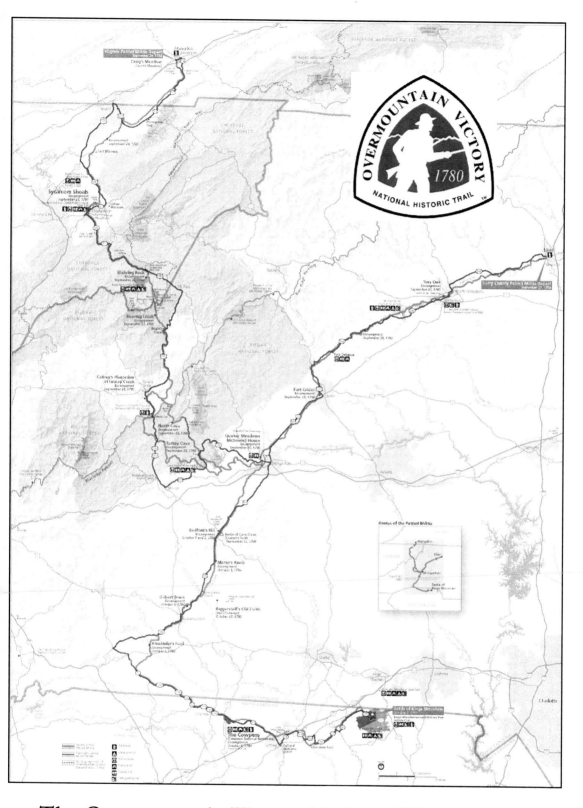

The Overmountain Victory National Historic Trail

A GUIDE TO THE OVERMOUNTAIN VICTORY NATIONAL HISTORIC TRAIL

Preface

Putting the story on the landscape

As with my books *In the Footsteps of Daniel Boone* and *In the Footsteps of Davy Crockett*, I try to help the reader experience history by putting the story on the landscape. As I often tell my audiences, I cannot take you back in time, but I can take you to the places where history happened, where events unfolded that made a difference in the lives of people and society. I think readers find that approach useful in appreciating the events in human history which have helped create the world as we understand it today.

The story of the backcountry Patriot militiamen who undertook a daunting task to campaign over the Appalachian Mountains, join with other militiamen from the Carolina Piedmont, and to pursue and confront and army of invaders is an account that begs to be retold on the landscape where it happened. That is the purpose of the **Overmountain Victory National Historic Trail** (OVNHT), to help visitors relive the history by following in the footsteps of these American Patriot heroes.

A Guide to the Overmountain Victory National Historic Trail leads visitors to the sites along the Trail where they can learn the story, experience the landscape, and imagine the historic events unfolding along the way. Among the many sites to be seen along the way, 34 are of particular interest. These are the sites identified during the creation of the OVNHT by the National Park Service during the early 1980s. In this *Guide*, an inset of the OVNHT logo is placed in the corner of a photo of each of certifiable sites depicted.

NPS Maps, the Trail, and the Motorized Route

The map of the Overmountain Victory National Historic Trail was created by the National Park Service and is in the public domain. I have used it in this guide in accordance with published policies. The *Guide* presents the Trail in 10 overlapping map panels, created for the convenience of the reader in following along the OVNHT. The map panels are all presented in the *Guide* at a consistent scale. The beginning and ending points of each of the 10 map segments were selected for convenience of display in this guide format. Another dividing of the OVNHT by the sequence of events would likely produce a much different dividing of the Trail.

The NPS map shows the historic route followed by the militiamen in their campaign to King's Mountain. Also shown on the map is the Motorized Route, which enables modern travelers to visit the OVNHT and follow the historic route with varying degrees of proximity by driving along primary highways. The *Guide* also refers to certified Trail segments which can be walked by the public. These segments can be within a one-mile wide corridor centered along the historic route. Walkable segments are added to the Trail each year as more partners join in its creation.

Before They Were Heroes at King's Mountain

Coincident with the release of *A Guide to the Overmountain Victory National Historic Trail* is the release of a larger treatment of the story told along the Trail. *Before They Were Heroes at King's Mountain* tells the story of the Overmountain and backcountry Patriot militia, their campaign over the mountain, their pursuit and defeat of Major Patrick Ferguson, and their withdrawal from the battlefield with their 800 prisoners. That book precedes that telling with accounts of events during the previous six years which engaged some of these same men in other campaigns and conflicts that prepared them for this confrontation with the invading British Legion. The story begins with Lord Dunmore's War in 1774 and the engagement of backcountry militiamen from Virginia. It includes the story of the first attempt by the British to carry out a Southern Strategy that resulted in the Battle of Moore's Creek Bridge in North Carolina. It also relates the accounts of the experience of the men of the western waters confronting Shawnees, Cherokees, and Chickamaugas in a contest for control of the land on which these native people had lived for centuries. In South Carolina, the story revolves primarily around the landing of General Clinton's British Legion in the spring of 1780 and Lord Cornwallis's march northward.

The full edition of *Before They Were Heroes at King's Mountain* is over 600 pages with 200 photographs and maps. For those readers interested in only part of the story, perhaps limited in its geography, three regional editions are available: Virginia, North Carolina/Tennessee, and South Carolina/Georgia. The maps on pages 105-108 show the events covered in each of the editions. All editions include the story of the muster, the march, the pursuit, the battle, and the aftermath of the campaign to and the battle at Little King's Mountain.

The Full Edition and the three regional editions are available from the publisher at *www.danielboonefootsteps.com.* Copies are also available at many of the visitor centers and

1774 to 1780

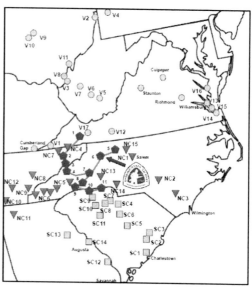

Available in **Full Edtion**
and three Regional Editions:
Virginia
North Carolina/Tennessee
SouthCarolina/Georgia

www.danielboonefootsteps.com

historic sites along the Overmountain Victory National Historic Trail.

This *Guide* includes a chapter excerpted from *Before They Were Heroes at King's Mountain.* Trail visitors may find the chapter "Three Friends on the Frontier" not only genuinely informative but quite surprising in its revelations. I hope you enjoy it.

Thank you for purchasing this *Guide*, for touring the Overmountain Victory National Historic Trail, and for valuing America's Revolutionary War history. Consider joining the Overmountain Victory Trail Association. (See *www.OVTA.org.*) Together we can preserve and protect the Trail, better interpret "The Story," and continue to promote broader and richer appreciation of America's history and heritage.

Recognizing 100 years of service.
National Park Service, 1916-2016

R.J., May 2011

Foreword

The Patriot victory at the Battle of Kings Mountain in October 1780 initiated a chain of events that ended with America's freedom. It had a profound effect on bringing about, at Yorktown, just twelve months and twelve days later, an end to the years-long American Revolution.

I have a deep, personal interest in the story of that battle and the Trail which commemorates the campaign that led to the battle. I grew up in my home town of Lenoir, North Carolina hearing stories of Kings Mountain. I knew some of the descendants of the heroes who fought in this battle. Fort Defiance, located in my home county of Caldwell, was the home of one of the heroes of the Battle of Kings Mountain, William Lenoir, who was a Captain at that time, and later rose to become the General of Militia for Western North Carolina.

But, my interest in the story and the Trail runs deeper still. In 1975, a remarkable group of dedicated men and women came to me as a Member of Congress. They asked me to become involved in seeking federal recognition of the route that was used by these early Patriots as they came out of the mountains to pursue the threatening British forces. This group also asked that we make every effort to preserve the route so that future generations of Americans could not only use the trail but embrace the history and see what hardships their ancestors had to surmount to win the victory that secured their Liberty.

The work we did together over the next five years culminated in the passage of federal legislation that I had sponsored. The bill was signed into law by President Jimmy Carter in August 1980, thus making the Overmountain Victory Trail a part of the National Historic Trails System. This Act provided for marking the Trail and took the initial steps to preserve the Trail for all time. Ever since the Trail was founded, significant steps have been taken to preserve the route. Moreover, the Overmountain Victory Trail Association is still alive and well, one of several dozen Trail partners supporting and collaborating with the National Park Service. The OVTA continues to tell the story of the Campaign and Battle of Kings Mountain all year-round, and especially during the annual reenactment of the heroic march each September and October.

**Senator James T. Broyhill introduced
federal legislation in 1977 to create
the Overmountain Victory National Historic Trail.**

This *Guide* to the Overmountain Victory National Historic Trail includes an excerpt from Randell's book, *Before They Were Heroes at King's Mountain*. That book tells the story of the battle and campaign, but more importantly it emphasizes the stories of these early American Patriots and the surprising connections they had to each other and to prior events that affected their preparedness for and their participation in the campaign to what became the Battle of Kings Mountain.

This *Guide* leads today's visitors along the Overmountain Victory National Historic Trail and the chapter "Overmountain Victory, 1780" shares the story (more briefly than his book) of those Patriots' experiences in getting to the site of the battle. This is the story of the brave men who mustered at Sycamore Shoals in pursuit of Major Patrick Ferguson and were joined in the effort by backcountry Patriots from North Carolina, South Carolina, and Georgia. This is America's story.

Randell Jones has made a most worthwhile contribution to the telling of American history. If you love America and if you like a good story, his book and this *Guide* are for you. I am proud to recommend his book and this *Guide* to all who have an interest in the early history of our country, and trust both will do much to keep alive the story of the victory at the Battle of Kings Mountain in the war that won for us all our Freedoms as Americans.

Senator James T. Broyhill of North Carolina
Former Member of Congress, 1963-1987

Overmountain Victory Trail Association

We keep **The Story** alive!

The story of the Overmountain Men and their campaign to the Battle of Kings Mountain is a story of the American Spirit. Faced with a threat to invade their Overmountain homelands, men and women of pioneer stock and frontier spunk rallied to the cause. They left their homes already at peril to renegade Cherokees and crossed over the mountains to answer the threat of Major Patrick Ferguson and the advancing British Legion.

The Overmountain Men along with other Patriots from the Piedmont sections of North Carolina, South Carolina and Georgia took the initiative to meet the threat head on. During two weeks, they pursued Patrick Ferguson's army of Loyalists, catching them atop Little Kings Mountain on October 7, 1780. In a monumental battle, this band of experienced militiamen—but still only citizen farmers, hunters, shopkeepers, and tradesmen—defeated Patrick Ferguson and forced the retreat of Lord Cornwallis and the most powerful army in the world.

Nearly two centuries later, in 1975, a group of private citizens began efforts to see the campaign route to the Battle of Kings Mountain designated as a National Historic Trail. With the partnership and efforts of U.S. Senator James T. Broyhill of North Carolina, this was accomplished in 1980. The Overmountain Victory National Historic Trail became the first such trail east of the Mississippi River and is today one of an elite number of historic trails in the country. During their early efforts to achieve this coveted designation, these citizens organized the Overmountain Victory Trail Association, chartered in 1977.

Since its inception, the OVTA has been keeping alive the story of the Campaign to the Battle of Kings Mountain. The OVTA has retraced the daily steps of the heroes on this campaign every year since 1975. This annual event continues to grow. Our band of commemorative marchers and reenactors moves down the Trail, encamping in the same locations on the same dates of the calendar as the Patriot militia did in 1780. During the march each year, OVTA educates the public. In the past two years alone, OVTA has told The Story to over 21,000 people during this annual commemorative march along the Trail corridor. Most are students learning firsthand that history teaches important values essential to what it means to be an American. They learn about how people lived two centuries ago and why some of them made the choices they did, choices that still benefit all Americans today.

We invite you to join in our effort. Join the Overmountain Victory Trail Association and help us keep the story alive. Visit us online at *www.OVTA.org* and become a member today.

Sincerely,

Alan Bowen
President, Overmountain Victory Trail Association, Inc.
www.OVTA.org

How To Use This Guide

This trail guide helps the heritage tourist explore and experience the Overmountain Victory National Historic Trail.

Visitors should first read the Preface, Foreword, and Introduction.

Next, visitors should read "The Overmountain Victory, 1780" to understand better the story interpreted by monuments, markers, plaques, wayside exhibits, replica forts, cabins, museums, historic sites and the landscape all along the Trail.

Each Map Panel provides information about the sites along the way and shares the story in more detail. The first half of the story unfolds from north to south along the Trail, but sites need not be visited in order. Events after the battle went south to north.

"Planning Your Visit" provides information about driving distances and time. It also suggests the types of learning opportunities and experiences available at each site. It identifies restrooms and services where available. This resource will help you plan and enjoy your visit to the OVNHT. All the communities along the Trail have more to share with you. Local visitor bureaus and chambers of commerce can point you to the sights and sites they have to share.

Visitors will enjoy learning more about the campaign of the Overmountain Men and battle by reading *Before They Were Heroes at King's Mountain*. Copies are available at sites along the Trail. An excerpted chapter, "Three Friends on the Frontier," is included in this *Guide* to give you a taste of the book. Copies can also be ordered online at *www.danielboonefootsteps.com* or by writing to Daniel Boone Footsteps, 1959 N. Peace Haven Road, # 105, Winston-Salem, NC 27106.

As you experience the OVNHT by using this *Guide*, please share your thoughts and suggestions on how to improve this trail guide by contacting the publisher at *DBooneFootsteps@gmail.com*.

Contents

Preface   ix

Foreword   xiii

How To Use This Guide   ixx

Contents   xxi

Introduction   1

Map Panels

    Map Panel # 1: Abingdon to Choate's Ford   3

    Map Panel # 2: Choate's Ford to Gap Creek   9

    Map Panel # 3: Gap Creek to Roaring Creek   13

    Map Panel # 4: Roaring Creek to North Cove
        and Turkey Cove   17

    Map Panel # 5: North Cove and Turkey Cove
        to Quaker Meadows   21

    Map Panel # 6: Elkin Creek to Fort Defiance   25

    Map Panel # 7: Fort Defiance to Quaker Meadows 31

    Map Panel # 8: Quaker Meadows to Gilbert Town   35

    Map Panel # 9: Gilbert Town to The Cowpens   39

    Map Panel # 10: The Cowpens to King's Mountain 43

The Overmountain Victory, 1780   47

Planning Your Visit   67

Excerpt from *Before They Were Heroes at King's Mountain*
    "Three Friends on the Frontier"   85

Introduction

"[The victory at Kings Mountain] was the joyful annunciation
of that turn of the tide of success
which terminated the Revolutionary War,
with the seal of our independence."
– Thomas Jefferson, 1822

The American Revolution Comes South

After five years of fighting to a stalemate in the New England and mid-Atlantic states, the British once again attempted their Southern strategy to stop the rebel uprising known as the American Revolution. Following a successful British siege in the spring of 1780, the surrender of Charlestown, South Carolina, in May led to the advance of General Lord Cornwallis's British Legion northward through South Carolina. August brought the disastrous defeat of the Continental Army's Southern Department (reconstituted under General Horatio Gates) at the Battle of Camden. Marching on toward Charlotte Town, Cornwallis looked unstoppable until the commander of his western flank, Major Patrick Ferguson, a Scotsman, imprudently threatened to invade and destroy the Overmountain regions of North Carolina and Virginia. In a response characteristic of their nature, a band of frontier militiamen — descendants of Scots-Irish, Welsh, German, and French Huguenot ancestry, among others — and without a single Continental soldier or Continental officer among them, amassed a fighting force of 2,000 men to pursue and defeat the threatening invaders. Their unexpected victory atop Little King's Mountain on October 7 stunned the British Legion and halted Cornwallis's advance northward for three months. The victory quelled the enthusiasm of Southern Loyalists and renewed the spirit of the Whig rebels in the South. It led to a succeeding string of victories that ended with Cornwallis's surrender at Yorktown just twelve months and twelve days after the Battle of Kings Mountain. The victory at King's Mountain was, in modern slang, a game-changer.

Overmountain Victory National Historic Trail

The story of the battle is commemorated and interpreted today by the National Park

Service at Kings Mountain National Military Park straddling the Cherokee/York county line in South Carolina. The story of the muster, the march, and the pursuit — that is, the campaign of the militiaman that created that confrontation at King's Mountain — is commemorated and interpreted by the National Park Service along the 330 miles of the Overmountain Victory National Historic Trail (OVNHT). The modern Trail follows closely the historic route, and stretches across four states. The western leg begins in Abingdon, Virginia, passes over the Appalachian Mountains along the border of East Tennessee and North Carolina, and descends the eastern face of the Blue Ridge Mountains. Following the Catawba River, it reaches Quaker Meadows in Morganton, North Carolina, where it is joined by the eastern leg running along the Yadkin River from Elkin, North Carolina. From Morganton, the OVNHT continues southward to Rutherfordton and then into Polk County before abruptly turning east-southeast. It crosses into South Carolina where it runs to Cowpens National Battlefield, then north of Gaffney, South Carolina, and on to Kings Mountain National Military Park.

The OVNH Trail, created in 1980 by federal legislation, became the first national historic trail east of the Mississippi River and took its place alongside the Lewis & Clark Trail and the Oregon Trail as a significant resource for recounting and memorializing an essential part of America's history and

heritage. Scores of organizations and thousands of individuals are partners with the OVNH Trail in supporting its charge to continually tell The Story of the heroes of King's Mountain.

This guide helps you follow along with these American patriots and learn about their courage, determination, and commitment that helped turn the tide of America's fight for freedom more than two and a quarter centuries ago.

Welcome to the
Overmountain Victory
National Historic Trail.

Abingdon to Choate's Ford

September 24 - 25

Map Panel #1

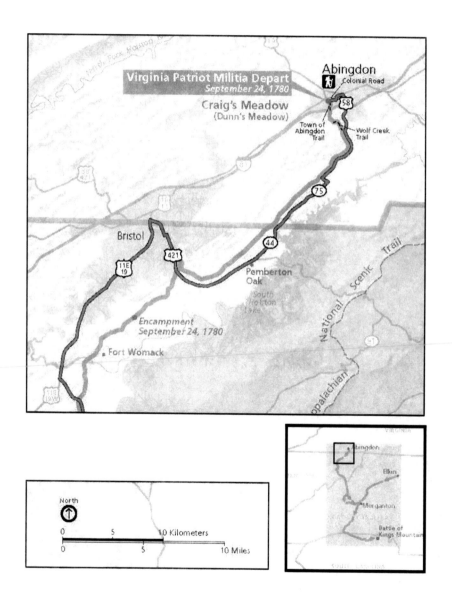

Abingdon to Choate's Ford

The Grave of William Campbell is a certified site of the OVNHT. It is on private property, but visitors are welcome. (This site is not shown on Map Panel #1.) It is located in Seven Mile Ford, Virginia near Exit 39 on I-81, about 25 miles northeast of Abingdon. From US 11 in Seven Mile Ford, find Seven Mile Ford Road parallel to the highway and across the railroad tracks. The driveway to the hilltop Apenvale cemetery is one-half mile west of the railroad crossing and immediately west of Spring Branch Rd. A wayside exhibit at the walled cemetery interprets Campbell's eventful, but short, life. A monument for **Aspenvale, Campbell's home**, is a few hundred feet farther west on Seven Mile Ford Road.

Colonel William Campbell was the general commander of the Patriot militia forces at King's Mountain. He was highly active in repressing Tory activity in southwest Virginia before he joined with Isaac Shelby and John Sevier in mustering men at Sycamore Shoals for the campaign to King's Mountain. While garrisoned in Williamsburg,

Campbell met and married Elizabeth Henry, a sister of Patrick Henry. Later that year, Campbell participated in removing royal governor Lord Dunmore from Virginia. After the victory at King's Mountain, he led troops at the Battle of Guilford Courthouse. In the summer of 1781, he was leading Virginia militiamen under the command of Marquis de La Fayette and marching toward Yorktown when he took ill. He died a few days later at age 36.

The Muster Grounds and the W. Blair Keller, Jr. Interpretive Center are located at 702 Colonial Road in Abingdon, Virginia. (See photo on page 51.) Virginia highway historical marker, "King's Mountain Men," is at Colonial Road and US Hwy 11/19 about one mile north of I-81 at Exit 14. Another highway historical marker is on Colonial Road opposite the Muster Grounds. A third marker honoring Virginia's militiamen is in the field at the Muster Grounds. A wayside exhibit for Retirement, the antebellum home adjacent to the grounds, is nearby.

South of the Muster Grounds on Stonemill Road (interesection is 200 yards

Historical markers, an informational kiosk, and the W. Blair Keller, Jr. Interpretive Center help inform visitors about events at the Muster Grounds in Abingdon, Virginia.

east on Colonial Road) near the underpass beneath I-81 is the site of Stone Mill on Wolf Creek. This segment of the OVNHT is along the route taken by the Washington County Militia marching south to Sycamore Shoals. Interpretive waysides at the pull-off from the road and along the trail interpret the route of the Virginia militiamen and the mill built after the Revolutionary War. Abingdon is home to many other sites of historical interest. (See *Planning Your Visit.*)

Abingdon to Choate's Ford

The Virginia militiamen followed the Watauga Road. For modern travelers, VA Hwy 75 generally parallels this route and leads south from Abingdon into Tennessee where it becomes TN Hwy 44. The remnant trunk of the **Pemberton Oak**, a certified site on the OVNHT, is at 1152 Pemberton Road, about 100 yards from the highway historical marker on US Hwy 421. The marker on US Hwy 421 is about 100 yards west from the intersection with TN Hwy 44. (This tree remnant is on private property. Please view it from the road only.) Captain John Pemberton mustered his militiamen beneath this spreading oak in 1780. It had been used for many years as such a gathering place for other militia. The tree, the last living thing on the Trail from

the era of the campaign and battle, survived into the early 21st century. A commemorative plaque is strapped to the massive trunk.

Bristol, Tennessee is the site of several interesting markers and locations related to the story of the Overmountain Men. One is the site of Sapling Grove, also called Shelby's Fort, the home of Colonel Isaac Shelby. A marker for the site of Shelby's Fort is at the corner of

Anderson Street and 7th Street. Another plaque for the site is attached to a building at the corner of 7th Street and Shelby Street. (See additional photos on page 50.) A **2009 marker**, commemorating Isaac Shelby, stands on Shelby Street a few paces east of 7th Street.

The site of **Womack's Fort** is on private property and not available for public access. The site is

commemorated by a Tennessee highway historical marker on TN Hwy 390 at Silver Grove Rd., immediately north of the bridge over the South Fork of Holston River at Bluff City, Tennessee.

About one-half mile east of TN Hwy 390 on Silver Grove Road is **Choate's Ford**, immediately downstream of the railroad crossing. The historic route followed by the Virginia Militia in 1780 passes through Bluff City on both private and public property.

Bluff City has created the Choate's Ford Walking Trail with a **pedestrain suspension bridge** spanning the river and enabling visitors to see the ford and South Fork Holston

Abingdon to Choate's Ford

River from two sides and to visit the **Choate's Ford wayside**.

A pull off and **information kiosk for the OVNHT** are on East Main Street near the river. It provides access to the foot bridge. A wayside exhibit shows the historic route and the OVNHT route, which is **marked on city sidewalks** through town.

A **commemorative marker for Choate's Ford**, erected by the OVTA (Overmountain Victory Trail Association) in 1998, stands in a public park across the river from the Womack's Old Fort marker.

Choate's Ford to Gap Creek
September 24 - 26

Map Panel #2

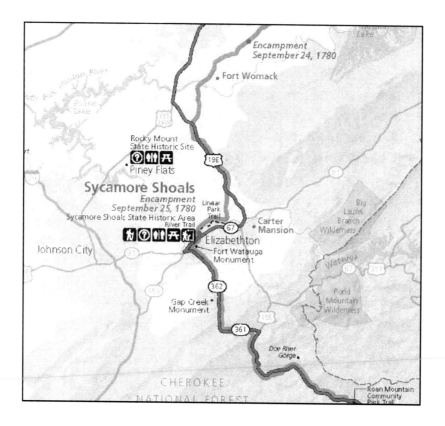

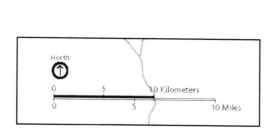

Choate's Ford to Gap Creek

Just as did the men under Captain John Pemberton, militiamen gathered from other parts of Sullivan and Washington counties in North Carolina. Some mustered at the home of William Cobb on the night of September 24, 1780 before continuing on to Sycamore Shoals. Cobb and his sons went along. The William Cobb home, living history programs, and a splendid museum are pre-

sented at **Rocky Mount Museum State Historic Site** on US Hwy 19E at Hyder Hill Road in Piney Flats, Tennessee, between Bluff City and Johnson City. This is a certified

site on the OVNHT. An admission fee is charged for this museum and its programming. The museum displays one of **Mary Patton's kettles** used in making gunpowder and interprets the interesting and dangerous art of its manufacture.

Nearby in Winged Deer Park, but not on the OVNHT, is the relocated **cabin of Robert**

Young, the man credited with shooting Major Patrick Ferguson at King's Mountain. The park and cabin are two miles south of Rocky Mount Museum on US Hwy 11W/19.

Adjacent to the cabin is the **Henry Massengil Monument**, commemorating the westward movement of pioneers into the "First Frontier," the East Tennessee Overmountain region. The 1937 monument was relocated to the park in 1990. Henry Massengil's wife was a sister to William Cobb. Entering the region in 1769, they were among its earliest pioneer settlers.

The Virginians and others coming from the north crossed the Watauga River at Sycamore Shoals. They gathered in the meadows surrounding Fort Watauga with other militiamen and some families coming from their own homes. The history of the Overmountain region and Fort Watauga is interpreted at **Sycamore Shoals State Historic Area** on US Hwy 321 (TN Hwy 67) in Elizabethton, Tennessee. A replica fort interprets the history and serves as the setting for reenactments and seasonal theatrical outdoor dramas. A museum, a movie, and bookstore in the visitor center offer generous opportunities for exploration and learning.

Another of the four kettles known to be used by Mary Patton to make gunpowder is displayed at Sycamore Shoals State Historic Area. The grave of Mary Patton, who provided 500 pounds of gunpowder to the Overmountain Men for their expedition is in the Patton-Simmons Cemetery, about 1.5 miles south of Milligan College after turning onto Toll Branch Road. It is a certified site on the OVNHT. (See photo on page 51.)

A certified segment of the OVNHT with interpretive wayside exhibits passes along the south bank of the Watauga River at the state historic area, indicating in one spot the **ford at Sycamore Shoals**. (See additional photo on page 52.)

Choate's Ford to Gap Creek

The **site of the original Fort Watauga** is commemorated a few blocks away on West G Street at Monument Avenue. From the exit of Sycamore Shoals State Historic Area, cross Elk Ave. immediately to Parkway Blvd. and proceed south for 0.2 mile. Turn right (southwest) for 0.9 mile to the monument. For a time, the fort was also known as Carter's Fort. Colonel John Carter was an early settler of the area and president of the Watauga Association, formed in 1772 by the Overmoutain residents to provide for their own governance. The **Carter Mansion** was

built before 1780 by John Carter and his son Landon Carter. The mansion and the family cemetery are

on the opposite side of Elizabethton from Fort Watauga monument. They are on Broad Street about 100 yards east of US Hwy 19E. Tours are available through the visitor center at Sycamore Shoals State Historic Area. Carter County is named for Landon Carter; Elizabethton is named for his wife, Elizabeth.

From the Fort Watauga monument, continue southwest for 0.4 miles to TN Hwy 362. Turn left and follow the OVNHT beside Gap Creek along the historic route taken by the Overmountain militiamen toward Yellow Mountain Gap. A **stone monument along Gap Creek** was erected by stu-

dents in 1976 during America's Bicentennial celebration. The school has since been razed, but the monument remains. It is 4.0 miles south along TN Hwy 362 from West G Street.

Gap Creek to Roaring Creek
September 26 - 28

Map Panel # 3

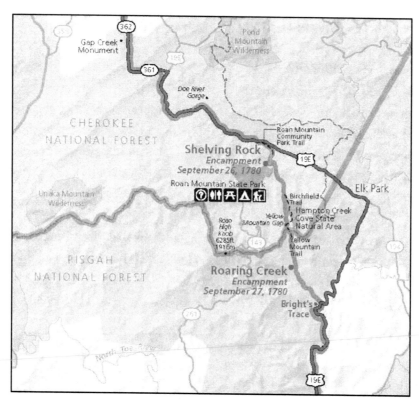

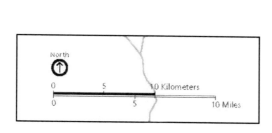

Gap Creek to Roaring Creek

The OVNHT along Gap Creek continues from TN Hwy 362/361 onto US Hwy 19E, where it continues south and east toward Roan Mountain, Tennessee and passes through the Doe River gorge. In the town of Roan Mountain, US Hwy 19E intersects with TN Hwy 143. A certified seg-

ment of the OVNHT runs along the **Doe River** in a community park there.

TN Hwy 143 leads south from US Hwy 19E to Roan Mountain State Park. Shelving Rock, a certified site, is adjacent to TN Hwy 143 after rounding a sharp curve about one mile from US Hwy 19E. A narrow pull-off is available, but approaching traffic is blind to your presence. It is dangerous to stop here. It is **not** recommended that you do so. A plaque was placed at Shelving Rock in 1910 by the John Sevier Chapter, Daughters of the American Revolution. Road construction partially filled in the rock overhang which would have been much deeper in 1780 than it is presently. (See photo on page 53.)

Across from Shelving Rock is the meadow called **"the Resting Place."** The Resting Place was the first level ground with water which accommodated travelers coming west after crossing Roan Mountain. The Overmountain militiamen camped in this field along Doe River on September 26, 1780. Currently the land is privately owned. A sign erect-

ed by the land owner at a paved pull-off gives details about the history of the site.

A certified segment of the OVNHT passes through the **Hampton Creek Cove State Natural Area**. This trail passes through state conservation land and onto US Forest Service land as the OVNHT approaches Yellow Mountain Gap. (See additional photo on page 53.) The historic route followed by the militiamen passes through an adjacent draw along Sugar Hollow Creek. The trailhead in Hampton Creek Cove Natural Area is on Hampton Creek Road about three miles off Old TN143 off TN Hwy 143. Old TN 143 is between Shelving Rock and US Hwy 19E.

At Yellow Mountain Gap, the OVNHT crosses the Appalachian Trail and passes from Tennessee into North Carolina. (In 1780, the state of Tennessee did not exist. The Overmountain region was in North Carolina.) The approach of the OVNHT from the west side includes remnants of a wagon road which would have been used in post-Revolutionary times to cross the mountains. In 1780, the route, known as Bright's Trace on both sides of the mountain, was a packhorse trail, a path likely made by deer, elk, and bison migrating over the mountains and later used by Cherokees and early settlers in moving through the area.

After arriving at Yellow Mountain Gap, the militia officers paraded their men in snow reported as "shoe-mouth deep" and had the men fire their weapons. While there, they discovered that two men, known to have leanings toward the Loyalists, were missing. The militiamen suspected the pair of stealing off to warn Ferguson of their militia gathering.

Passing east from **Yellow Mountain Gap**, the OVNHT descends along **Roaring Creek** and passes by a spot where the militiamen camped on the night of September 27, 1780. A plaque was placed by the Daughters of the American Revolution to commemorate this **camp site** along an unpaved section of Roaring Creek Road on US Forest Service land. The plaque was removed by parties unknown around 2007; the rock base remains.

The **Yellow Mountain Road on the east side of the mountain** is marked at the intersection of Roaring Creek Road at US Hwy 19E. (See photo on page 54.) US Hwy 19E continues south along the North Toe River toward Spruce Pine, North Carolina.

Roaring Creek to North Cove
and Turkey Cove
September 28 - 29

Map Panel # 4

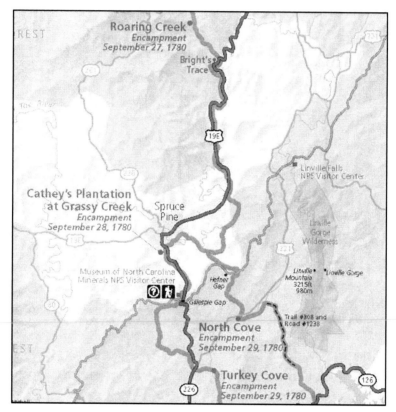

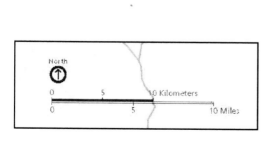

Roaring Creek to North Cove and Turkey Cove

The OVNHT follows US Hwy 19E and the North Toe River south from Yellow Mountain Road and Roaring Creek along the Blue Ridge plateau. Near Spruce Pine are two certified sites related to the story of the Overmountain Men after the battle. Both are on private land; access is restricted. One is **Davenport Springs** along Bright's Trace. The militiamen passed this site on their way to the battle and afterward on their return home. The **grave of Captain Robert Sevier**, who succumbed to his battle wound while stopped at the springs nine days after the battle, is nearby. It is a certified site. (See photo on page 65.)

US Hwy 19E departs from the historic route and continues southward into Spruce Pine. On the night of September 28, 1780, the militiamen camped on the south side of the North Toe River near the mouth of Grassy Creek. The site, also known as Cathey's Plantation, is about a mile south of Spruce Pine. The exact site, privately owned, is not identified, but a marker was placed in 1910 by the John Sevier Chapter, Daughters of the American Revolution, in the town of Spruce Pine. The DAR marker is at the train depot on Locust Street. (See photo on page 394, *Before They Were Heroes at King's Mountain.*)

On September 29, the Overmountain militiamen proceeded up Grassy Creek to the crest of the Blue Ridge Mountains at **Gillespie Gap**. That site is marked by a plaque on the grounds of the **Museum of North Carolina Minerals**, a National Park Service facility on the Blue Ridge Parkway at Mile Post 331. The route is followed today by NC Hwy 226 from Spruce Pine. (See additional photos on page 54.) An **exhibit in the museum** interprets the OVNHT.

After making the difficult decision to split their forces to descend the mountains on separate paths, one party marched back to Cathey's Plantation and then proceeded up the North Toe River and today's Little Rose Creek to reach Hefner Gap at Mile Post 326 on the Blue Ridge Parkway. It is a half-mile east of McKinney Gap. McKinney Gap can be seen from The Loops overlook on the Blue Ridge Parkway at Mile Post 328. (See photo on page 55.) These militiamen reached the far ridgeline observable from Mile Post 326 and descended into the North Fork Catawba River valley and

camped at **North Cove** near the mouth of Hunnycut's (Honeycutt) Creek. That site along US Hwy 221 is not marked, but North Cove School Road, connecting US Hwy 221 and Old Linville Road in a half-mile stretch, passes over Hunnycut's Creek and North Fork Catawba River in a broad meadow where the militiamen likely camped. At that camp, Shelby's and Sevier's men were found by Colonel Charles McDowell who rode out from his home at Quaker Meadows to bring them news.

The trailhead for US Forest Service Trail # 308 into the Pisgah National Forest (a certified segment of the OVNHT) departs Old Linville Road 2.3 miles north of North Cove School Road.

The other half of the militiamen, under William Campbell, descended the east face of the Blue Ridge Mountains from Gillespie Gap to reach Turkey Cove. The safer descent from the Blue Ridge Parkway for modern travelers is along NC Hwy 226; however, the historic route descended by a route departing from Little Switzerland (farther west from Gillespie Gap along NC Hwy 226) approximated by NC Hwy 226A. Modern travelers should use that extremely winding route cautiously, if at all. It is **not** recommended.

The Turkey Cove camp site is not marked but is known to be along Armstrong Creek. This would be near the intersection of US Hwy 221 and NC Hwy 226. It is the **bottomland of Armstrong Creek** as it flows into the North Fork Catawba River. This camp site may well have been where Old US Hwy 221 intersects American Thread Road. Or, the site could have been the land along Armstrong Creek one mile west and at the southwest corner of US Hwy 221 and NC Hwy 226. In any case, the landscape would have looked much different in 1780 from what is viewed today, although the general landform is the same.

North Cove and Turkey Cove to Quaker Meadows

September 30

Map Panel # 5

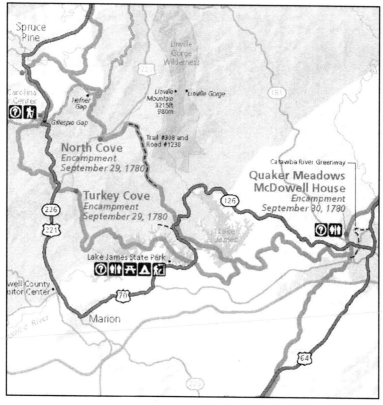

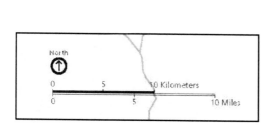

North Cove and Turkey Cove to Quaker Meadows

Along the OVNHT east of North Cove, a certified segment of the Trail passes through US Forest Service land in the Pisgah Forest along **Trail # 308** and Road # 1238. This

route departs Old Linville Road (parallel to US Hwy 221) and north of North Cove near the mouth of Bridge Branch. Trail # 308 climbs southeast to the ridge of Linville Mountain where that route becomes part of North Carolina's Sea-to-Mountain Trail, crossing the Yellow Fork watershed, dropping and recovering about 300 feet in elevation. The OVNHT segment then follows and parallels Road # 1238 (an unpaved road

called Kistler Memorial Highway) along the ridge line separating Paddy's Creek to the west and Shook Creek to the east. Additional directions for locating these routes on US Forest Service Land can be found at the US Forest Service office at Exit 90 along I-40 in McDowell County, North Carolina.

Another certified segment of the OVNHT follows Paddy's Creek at Lake James State Park. The segment is accessible off NC Hwy 126 north of Lake James in Burke County.

In Marion, along the Motorized Route of the OVNHT and near the intersection of US Hwy 221 and US Hwy

70, stands **the home of Joseph McDowell**, which he called Pleasant Gardens. (This is not Joseph McDowell of Quaker Meadows, the brother of Charles McDowell. Joseph McDowell of Pleasant Gardens, a cousin, also commanded men at the Battle of Kings Mountain.) His home is a certified site on the OVNHT.

History Worth Knowing

A dozen years after the end of the American Revolution, Joseph McDowell of Pleasant Gardens died. In 1797, his widow, Mary Moffitt McDowell, married John Carson who lived two miles west on the Catawba River (at today's Historic Carson House). She took with her the name of her home and called her new home with Carson by the same, Pleasant Gardens. (Some of John Carson's escapades with Patrick Ferguson are recounted on pages 373-4, *Before They Were Heroes at King's Mountain*.) She gave birth in 1798 to a son, Samuel Price Carson. He was elected to Congress in 1825. His reelection campaign in 1827 was a bitter contest with the man he had unseated. Carson killed his opponent, Robert Brank Vance, in a duel, witnessed on November 5 by newly-elected Tennessee Congressman David Crockett. Crockett was a friend of the Carson family as his second wife, Elizabeth, was from Swannanoa, North Carolina. Her father, Robert Patton, had helped organize some of the efforts in which John Carson participated to keep the cattle of Whig rebels safe in 1780 from Ferguson's forag-

ing parties. That participation—depending on conflicting interpretations—was the cause of the duel to defend John Carson's honor.

After finishing their separate political careers in Congress, in 1835 David Crockett and Sam Carson each made his way to Texas. Crockett was killed at the Alamo on March 6, 1836. A week later, Carson was nearly elected president of the new Republic of Texas, but instead served for a time as Secretary of State for the Republic during the Texas Revolution.

Remarkably, a half-century before, in the fall of 1780, not so far from the Pleasant Gardens home of Joseph McDowell on the Catawba River in today's Marion, the Overmountain militiamen were passing through the wilderness, some on horseback, some on foot, in pursuit of Major Patrick Ferguson. Among the ranks of those mustered under Colonel John Sevier was a man who had moved to the Overmountain region seeking good land at a good price —John Crockett. He became the father six years later of the boy who would become that colorful Tennessee Congressman who would live on as an American frontier legend. (See *In the Footsteps of Davy Crockett*.)

Dr. Robert Brank Vance would have been an uncle to Zebulon Vance (b. 1830), North Carolina's governor during the Civil War. The doctor's father, David Vance, fought at King's Mountain. Zebulon Vance later served as US Senator from North Carolina and as the defense attorney for Tom Dula, accused and hanged for killing Laura Foster. (*Hang Down Your Head, Tom Dooley.*) Dula's grave is along the Yadkin River, not far from where the Surry and Wilkes militiamen camped on the night of September 29, 1780.) The grave of Laura Foster is visible from NC Hwy 268 across from a marker 4.0 miles south of the Wilkes/Caldwell county line and four miles north of Fort Defiance.

After rejoining forces along the Catawba River on September 30, the Overmountain militiamen continued east in that valley to reach Quaker Meadows and the homes of Colonel Charles McDowell and his brother, Major Joseph McDowell. The existing 1812 home of Charles McDowell, a certified site on the OVNHT, is owned by Historic Burke Foundation. It is located on St. Mary's Church

Rd. just off NC Hwy 181 west of Morganton. Nothing remains of the McDowell home of 1780. (See photo on page 55.)

The officers met in council on the night of September 30 beneath the branches of what was called the **Council Oak**. A marker on NC Hwy 181 (N. Green Street) at Bost Road commemorates this oak, long since gone. (See photo of marker on page 56.) Quaker Meadows is occupied today by a golf course and commercial development along NC Hwy 181.

Quaker Meadows Cemetery, a certified site of the OVNHT, is the burial site of Charles McDowell and Joseph McDowell among many others of the 18th century. This gated, hilltop cemetery is located across NC Hwy 181 from the Charles McDowell House. It is at the end of Branstrom Drive,

off Sam Wall Ave., off Independence Blvd. (NC Hwy 126), off N. Green Street (NC Hwy 181.) Freedom Park is on Independence Blvd. at Sam Wall Ave. OVTA marchers fire a commemorative volley at the cemetery annually on the morning of October 1.

Elkin Creek to Fort Defiance

September 27 - 28

Map Panel # 6

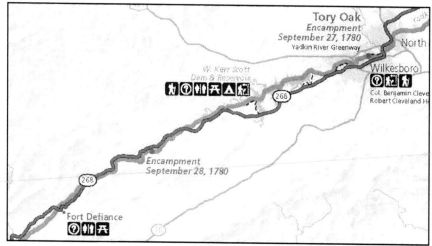

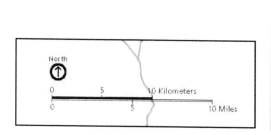

Elkin Creek to Fort Defiance

The eastern leg of the OVNHT begins at the **Mustering Ground**, the trailhead in Elkin, North Carolina. At this site, Surry County Militiamen under Major Joseph

Winston mustered and camped before their departure on September 27. Interpretive wayside exhibits sit at a paved pull-off overlooking Elkin City Park from NC Hwy 268. (See additional photo on page 56.) From here, about four miles of trail follows along Elkin Creek and continues upstream along the north side of the **Yadkin River**.

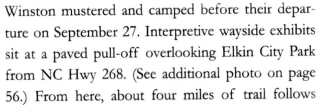

Along their march up the Yadkin River, the Surry militiamen passed the home of Colonel Benjamin Cleaveland. A highway historical marker on NC Hwy 268 south of Elkin in Ronda commemorates the site of his home, **The Round About**. Nothing remains of the Cleaveland home, and he later lost the land to a better title.

The combined militia forces of Colonel Cleaveland and Major Winston camped along the Yadkin River near the Tory Oak, in today's Wilkesboro. The **Tory Oak** is a certified site of the OVNHT and is adjacent to the Wilkes Heritage Museum. The original oak survived into the 1990s. It has been replaced by a planting. A wayside exhibit interprets the site and the tree's notorious history.

The **Wilkes Heritage Museum** hosts an extensive exhibit about the OVNHT and the campaign to the battle at King's Mountain. It also includes many additional exhibits about the history of the Upper Yadkin River Valley.

Near the museum is the **cabin of Robert Cleaveland**, brother of Colonel Benjamin Cleaveland, and a participant in the Battle of Kings Mountain. (Next to the cabin is the jail where Tom Dula was kept after his arrest for the murder of Laura Foster. See "History Worth Knowing" on page 23.)

Elkin Creek to Fort Defiance

The Cleaveland Cabin sits adjacent to a certified segment of the OVNHT connecting over a **pedestrian bridge** to the Trail. The OVNHT runs along the north bank of the Yadkin River in Wilkes County as part of the **Yadkin River Greenway**.

Also near the museum is a concrete **statue of Benjamin Cleaveland** with its own interesting art history.

Just southwest of Wilkesboro where US Hwy 421 crosses the river, **Moravian Creek** flows into the Yadkin River. Today, this point offers trailhead access to the Yadkin River Greenway. In 1780 after the battle, the victorious Patriots, marching their Tory prisoners toward Bethabara, camped at this site on the night of October 18 before fording the creek on the following morning and marching by the Tory Oak.

The march of the Wilkes and Surry militiamen up the Yadkin River valley in late September before the battle is interpreted at the **Visitor Assistance Center at W. Kerr Scott Reservoir**, a US Army Corps of Engineers site. A certified segment of the OVNHT winds along the east shore of the reservoir. Another segment follows along the west bank of the river below the dam from the Fish Dam Creek Overlook located at the west end of the dam.

The militiamen rode and marched along the **streambed valley now submerged**. Worth noting, they passed by, if not over, Holman's Ford, site of a cabin and homestead of Daniel Boone, built in 1766 and now also submerged beneath W. Kerr Scott Reservoir. (See *In the Footsteps of Daniel Boone.*) Benjamin Cleaveland may well have known Daniel

Boone personally. (See *Before They Were Heroes at King's Mountain*, pages 22-23.) **A replica of another Daniel Boone cabin** built in the area along Beaver Creek is on display at Whippoorwill Village on NC Hwy 268 near Ferguson.

Elkin Creek to Fort Defiance

Southwest of W. Kerr Scott Reservoir, **Mountain View Overlook** offers an elevated view of the Yadkin River valley to the northeast. From this spot, visitors can see the valley through which the Surry and Wilkes militiamen rode on September 27 and 28. It also offers a grand view of the Blue Ridge Mountains to the west. To reach this overlook, return to NC 268 from W. Kerr Scott Reservoir and turn south (right) for 5.3 miles to Boomer-Ferguson School Road. Turn right, then take the second left and again turn left immediately after 50 feet. Drive uphill 0.4 mile to the overlook.

On the night of September 28, the Surry and Wilkes militiamen camped along the **Yadkin River at the mouth of Elk Creek** (not to be confused with Elkin Creek). This site is near the Wilkes/Caldwell county line. The site is unmarked and on private property, but is a reasonable site for such an encampment. The militiamen would pass Fort Defiance early in the next day's ride.

Fort Defiance to Quaker Meadows
September 29 - 30

Map Panel # 7

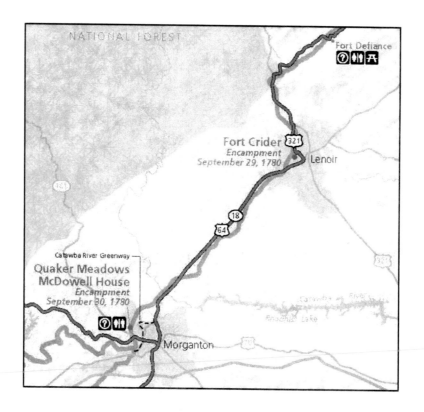

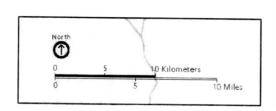

After making camp on September 28 along the Yadkin River, the Surry and Wilkes militia pressed on toward Quaker Meadows on September 29. They soon passed by **Fort Defiance**, the fortified home of Captain William Lenoir, one of their party.

Today, **Fort Defiance** is the later 1792 home of General William Lenoir, who fought at the Battle of Kings Mountain and afterward served the state of North

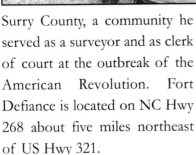

Carolina notably as a prominent and influential statesman and as the first president of the Board of Trustees of the University of North Carolina. This structure is named for the earlier fortified home he built nearby. He had lived closer to today's Wilkesboro when he first arrived in 1775 in what was then

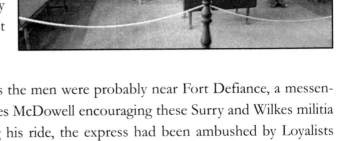

Surry County, a community he served as a surveyor and as clerk of court at the outbreak of the American Revolution. Fort Defiance is located on NC Hwy 268 about five miles northeast of US Hwy 321.

During this leg of the march as the men were probably near Fort Defiance, a messenger arrived from Colonel Charles McDowell encouraging these Surry and Wilkes militia to press on with haste. During his ride, the express had been ambushed by Loyalists attempting to thwart the mustering of the Patriot militia at Quaker Meadows.

On the night of September 29, the Wilkes and Surry militiamen camped at **Crider's Fort**, also called Gryder's Fort and Krider's Fort. That fort, built for protection against raids by Cherokees in the mid-1770s, was located in today's Lenoir, NC at the site of the former Lenoir High School (now private residences) on Willow Street between College and Harper avenues. The marker is at the corner of Willow Street and Harper Avenue.

On September 30, the Wilkes and Surry militiamen crossed over the **Johns River**, where US Hwy 64 crosses today, to reach Quaker Meadows. The OVNHT follows that route. A crossing of the Catawba

River at Rocky Ford is the site selected by the National Park Service in 2010 for establishing the future headquarters and a visitor center for the Overmountain Victory National Historic Trail.

A certified segment of the OVNHT follows the **Catawba River Greenway** along the east bank of the river and passes beneath the bridge farther south at NC Hwy 181 adjacent to Quaker Meadows. The 1780 militiamen, however, did not cross the Catawba River before reaching Quaker Meadows.

Historic Burke Foundation hosts an **annual commemorative event** at the McDowell House near the historic date of September 30 when the

Overmountain Men arrived at Quaker Meadows, a certified site, and were soon joined by the Surry County and Wilkes County militia who had come up the Yadkin River valley. **A wayside exhibit at the McDowell House** interprets the joining of militia forces.

Quaker Meadows to Gilbert Town

October 1 - 4

Map Panel # 8

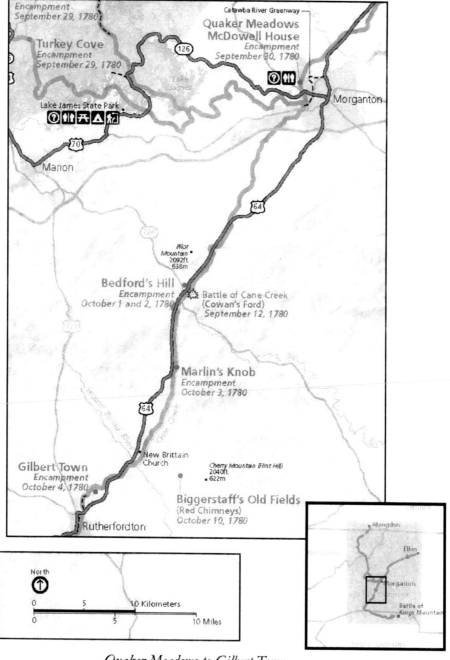

Quaker Meadows to Gilbert Town

From Quaker Meadows at today's Morganton, the combined force of some 1,400 militiamen from the Overmountain region and the Yadkin River valley proceeded south toward Gilbert Town, where they expected to find Major Patrick Ferguson and his

Loyalists. They crossed the Catawba River at **Greenlee Ford** and then passed through the Silver Creek watershed to a point near its head at Pilot Mountain. (Not to be confused with Pilot Mountain in Surry County.) Today's travelers follow US Hwy 64 south from Morganton and along **"Victory Trail" Highway**. At the Burke/McDowell county line on US Hwy 64, modern travelers pass through a saddle between the South Mountains on the east and Pilot Mountain on the west. This **saddle and Pilot Mountain** were the 18th-century guides leading the militiamen across the landscape. In passing south

through the saddle, travelers cross from the Catawba River basin into the Broad River basin. In 1780, the militiamen camped at Bedford Hill (not the same as Pilot Mountain), spreading out across the area and likely camping in the headwaters of both Silver Creek (Catawba River basin) and Cane Creek (Broad River basin). A turn onto Fortune Road affords good views of Pilot Mountain to the north and the headwaters of Silver Creek. (See photo on page 57.) Two hundred feet south of Fortune Road on US Hwy 64 is unpaved Bill Deck

Road to the west which passes over Bedford Hill to reach NC Hwy 226, which returns east to US Hwy 64. US Hwy 64 descends steeply to the south for a mile from Bedford

Hill through the rugged headwater area into the Cane Creek valley.

One mile south of NC Hwy 226 on US Hwy 64 is a highway historical marker commemorating the September 12, 1780 ambush of Ferguson's militiamen along Cane Creek by Patriot militiamen under Colonel Charles McDowell. (See photo on page 50.) In escaping the skirmish, McDowell and his men withdrew to the safety of the Overmountain region in the Watauga River valley. (Their presence was noted by Captain Joseph Martin, Virginia's Indian agent then living at the Long Island of the Holston. See page 377, *Before They Were Heroes at King's Mountain.*) They were there when word came to the region of Ferguson's threat to invade that area. As his militiamen mustered with those of Shelby, Sevier, and Campbell in the Overmountain region, Colonel Charles McDowell rode ahead to Quaker Meadows to recruit others and to prepare for the militia's arrival.

After camping two nights at Bedford Hill due to rainy weather, the militiamen were eager to move on. They departed on the morning of October 3 after spirited talks by colonels Cleveland and Shelby. The men followed Cane Creek south, parallel and adjacent to US Hwy 64, to their camp site along the creek beneath **Marlin's Knob**. On October 4th, the men continued south along Cane Creek. The OVNHT departs from US Hwy 64 at Cane Creek Road (not to be confused with Cane Creek Mountain Road) four miles south of NC Hwy 226. The Trail follows Cane Creek Road for about six miles through a picturesque, rural valley, where it intersects again with US Hwy 64. The

crooked route of the creek was challenging for the militiamen, even though the terrain was gently sloped. In a separate movement through this valley, a party of Loyalists reported crossing the supremely winding creek 19 times in four miles. (See page 372, *Before They Were Heroes at King's Mountain.*)

Near the mouth of Cane Creek at Second Broad River, the militiamen encountered Brittain Church, built in 1768. Modern travelers find New Brittain Church (built in 1852 and bricked in 1940) at the same site, eight miles south of the Cane Creek marker and seven miles northeast of Rutherfordton. (See photo on page 58.) During the later withdrawal from the battlefield, the militiamen left some of their wounded under the care of those in the community around Brittain Church. The **cemetery behind the church** includes the graves of more than a dozen Revolutionary War veterans, including some who did not survive wounds received at King's Mountain. (See page 482, *Before They Were Heroes at King's Mountain*.)

Modern travelers continue south along US Hwy 64 toward Rutherfordton to reach the site of **Gilbert Town**. Travelers have choices. Turn west on Oscar Justice Road and then south on Rock Road, or closer to Rutherfordton, turn north onto Old Gilbert Town Road to Rock Road about 100 yards west of the Gilbert Town markers. Alternatively, travelers can continue on US 64 to Alternate US Hwy 74 and then turn right onto Rock Road; the Gilbert Town markers are about two miles north.

Another certified site, Biggerstaff's Old Fields, is also related to the later withdrawal of the Patriot militiamen after the battle. Here on October 14, 1780, a week after the battle at King's Mountain, the Patriot militiamen held trials for many of the Loyalist prisoners. They condemned about 32 of the prisoners to hang for crimes allegedly committed against Patriots and Patriot families; they hanged nine Loyalists. The site of the encampment, trials, and hangings is commemorated today by a highway historical marker located near the community of Sunshine about

ten miles northeast of Ruth. Follow Green Street off Alternate US Hwy 74 in Rutherford/Ruth. Green Street is one-half mile south of US Hwy 64 on Alt. US Hwy 74. The Biggerstaff site is immediately west of today's Cherry Mountain, then known as Flint Hill. (See photo on page 65.) The scene of multiple hangings carried out by torchlight is depicted in **Louis Glanzman's painting** on display in the Tennessee State Museum in Nashville.

Gilbert Town to The Cowpens
October 4 - 6

Map Panel # 9

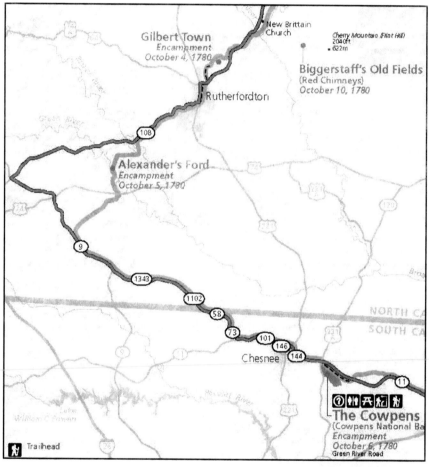

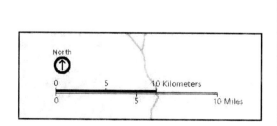

Gilbert Town to The Cowpens

The Patriot militiamen reached Gilbert Town on October 4, expecting to find Patrick Ferguson and his Loyalist forces camped there. Gilbert Town, established only the year before, was the first county seat of Rutherford County, carved and renamed by the Whig rebels from what the British called Tryon County. The site of Gilbert Town is on Rock Road, northeast of Rutherfordton and about two miles from the intersection of US Hwy 64 and Alt US Hwy 74. It is near the intersection of Rock Road and Old Gilberttown Road. (See photo on page 58.) During the American Revolution, this site was occupied at different times by Patriot militia, by Loyalist troops, and by General Lord Cornwallis.

Exhibits about the site and a display of artifacts removed from the site of Gilbert Town are in the lobby of the Rutherford County Office Building on N. Main Street.

The Patriots departed Gilbert Town on October 5, searching for the route Ferguson had taken in his retreat toward the safety of a larger British army. The Patriot militia pursued him into the watershed of the Broad River and the Green River, where they lost the trail. After riding all night from his camp near Flint Hill (today's Cherry Mountain) with information returned by a Patriot spy, Colonel Edward Lacey of the South Carolina militia found the militiamen at the ford on **Green River** and redirected them in pursuing Ferguson's retreating army.

Modern travelers along the Overmountain Victory National Historic Trail follow NC Hwy 108 southwest from Rutherfordton. The historic route can be followed off NC Hwy 108 onto unpaved (and sometimes unmarked) Simms Sandpit Road which becomes Grays Road until it reaches County Line Road. (Simms Sandpit Road is 3.8 miles from Alt US Hwy 221 on NC Hwy 108.) Alternatively, travelers can remain on NC Hwy 108 to County Line Road, then go south,

passing Grays Road and continuing a quarter-mile to Gray's Chapel. Access from this point to the ford on Green River, later called Alexander's Ford, is under development by Polk County as the Bradley Nature Preserve. Until then, the land is privately owned and is not open to visitors. A remnant of the historic route to the ford will be preserved in this planned development. (See photo on page 433, *Before They Were Heroes at King's Mountain*.)

The redirected Patriot militia, having divided their forces into mounted and foot soldiers, moved on the morning of October 6 to the south and out of the Green River valley to a ridgeline road, today's NC Hwy 9. Certified segments of the OVNHT are along Sandy Plains Road passing through the property of the White Oaks development on land given in 1743 by King George II to the family of Ambrose Mills, one of the Loyalists hanged at Biggerstaff's Old Fields. Another certified segment of the OVNHT

passes through **Overmountain Vinyards** at 2012 Sandy Plains Road.

Modern travelers leaving Grays' Chapel can turn west on Abrams Road from County Line Road. (The road is called Gray's Road in Rutherford County to the east and Abrams Road in Polk County to the west.) Follow Abrams Road for 4.8 miles to Pea Ridge Road making certain to turn south (left) after about 2.5 miles to continue on Abrams (& Moore) Road where it joins with Manus Chapel Road. Turn south (left) at Pea Ridge Road and cross over US Hwy 74 in a quarter mile. Continue on Pea Ridge Road. Pass entrance to White Oak development after 1.2 miles from US 74. At 2.25 miles from US 74, turn right onto Sandy Plains Road along which run segments of the OVNHT on White Oak development land and Overmountain Vinyards. Continue for 4.2 miles to NC Hwy 9. An alternative to avoid Sandy Plains Road would be to go west on US Hwy 74 to reach NC Hwy 9 and continue south, passing Sandy Plains Road within three miles.

Modern travelers follow NC Hwy 9 and other roads into South Carolina to reach **Cowpens National Battlefield**. From Sandy Plains Road, follow NC Hwy 9 for 2.9 miles and turn left onto Chesnee Road. Continue along this ridge road for 4.9 miles crossing into Rutherford County where the road becomes Mills Gap Road. Enter South Carolina after 1.6 miles where the road becomes Parris Bridge Road. Continue on that road and Arrowood Branch Road for 3.0 miles to reach SC Hwy

11. Continue east (left) on SC Hwy 11 for 3.5 miles to Chesnee and then 2.5 miles more to Cowpens National Battlefield. This is the site of The Cowpens, where the Overmountain Men and the Yadkin River valley militiamen joined up with the South Carolina militia under colonels

Edward Lacey and William Hill. Segments of the old road leading onto the battlefield are part of the Overmountain Victory National Historic Trail. (See photos on page 60.) **Exhibits in the visitor center** focus primarily on the battle fought at The Cowpens in January 1781 as Cornwallis renewed his effort to invade North Carolina following the defeat of Ferguson at King's Mountain three months earlier. The **annual OVTA reenactment march** includes commemoration activities at Cowpens National Battlefield on October 6.

The Cowpens to King's Mountain
October 6 - 7

Map Panel # 10

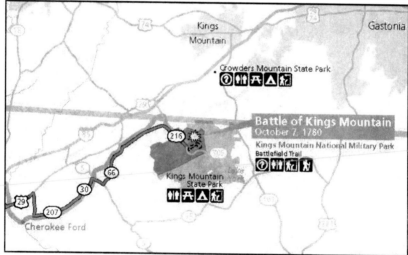

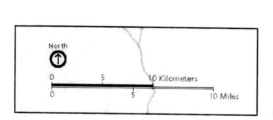

The Cowpens to King's Mountain

The Overmountain and backcountry militiamen arrived at The Cowpens **(Cowpens National Battlefield)** from the ford at Green River. They met up there with the South Carolina militiamen under colonels Lacey and Hill there. Together they numbered near 2,000. Receiving reports from returning scouts and spies, the combined Patriot militia force again divided its ranks. The officers selected a corps of 910 mounted militiamen to ride all night in an effort to catch Ferguson before he got any closer to Charlotte and the safety of General Lord Cornwallis's larger army of British Legion.

The historic route the mounted militiamen followed on that cold, rainy October night is approximated, in part, today by following SC Hwy 11 to I-85, Interstate 85 from Exit 92 to Exit 96, and then SC Hwy 329 to approach the Cherokee Ford. The OVNHT Motorized Route includes a route into Gaffney on SC Hwy 11 and then follows SC Hwy 18 (N. Limestone Street) northeast to parallel I-85 from Exit 95 to Exit 96.

In Gaffney, the reinterred **remains of Colonel James Williams and a monument** to him are on the front lawn of the Cherokee County Administration Building at 210 N. Limestone Street (SC Hwy 150.) (See photo on page 64.) Annually during the morning of October 7, OVTA marchers fire a commemorative volley at the grave site to honor

Colonel Williams, the highest ranking Patriot officer killed or mortally wounded at King's Mountain.

The historic route follows a ridge through the Cherokee Creek watershed, adjacent to today's Lake Whelchel, where a segment of the OVNHT follows along the south bank of the lake.

Upon reaching the Broad River, the militiamen suspected an ambush at the intended crossing and decided it more prudent to cross farther downstream at the Cherokee Ford. The Cherokee Ford, a certified site on the OVNHT, is off Ford Road off SC Hwy 329 about 1.5 miles south of US Hwy 29. (See photo on page 61.)

After reaching the east side of the Broad River at **Cherokee Ford**, the militiamen awaited an all-clear signal from their scout, Enoch Gilmer, that no ambush was laid on the east bank. According to 19th century historian Lyman C. Draper, Gilmer signaled them by singing verses from a jolly tune of the day, called *Barney Linn*. In 1978, Professor

Bobby Gilmer Moss of Limestone College discovered the likely words to that folk song that made its way to the American colonies with the Scots-Irish immigrants. It was likely based on a Scottish ballad, *Tom Bolynn*. The chorus went: "Tom Bolynn was a Scotch-man born/His shoes worn out, his stockings torn/The calf of his leg came down to his shin/A bulldog and panters*, said Tom Bolynn." ("Panters" was sometimes pronounced "painters" and referred to panthers, that is, eastern cougars.)

From Cherokee Ford, the militiamen followed a track across the northwest headwaters of Kings Creek, receiving information along the way that Ferguson was camped atop Little King's Mountain. Modern travelers can follow this route closely on secondary

state roads, following SC/SSR 30 from US Hwy 29, two miles east of Broad River. This route changes names from Cherokee Falls Road to Batchelor Drive to Oak Grove Road. At SC Hwy 5, turn southeast for one mile to SC/SSR 60, Jumping Branch Road. Go north to SC/SSR 21 (Antioch Road) and follow it east to SC Hwy 216, which leads south to Kings Mountain National Military Park. The route has **additional markers** on the way.

The Overmountain Victory National Historic Trail ends at the boundary of Kings Mountain National Military Park. The story of the battle is interpreted in the park on a **walking trail**

The Cowpens to King's Mountain

through the battlefield among many monuments and markers (see pages 62-63), and in the visitor center through a movie and extensive **exhibits in the museum**. The bookstore affords visitors the opportunity to immerse themselves further in learning about the American Revolution, especially the Southern Campaign.

The Overmountain Victory, 1780

Introduction

The rebellion of the American colonies began almost immediately after the end of the French and Indian War (1754-1763). Great Britain was in serious debt having engaged at length in a world war and Parliament needed to raise substantial revenue quickly. The colonists in the 13 English colonies vigorously protested the efforts of Parliament to tax them without representation. The shooting war, the actual American Revolution, began some ten years later with the "shot-heard-round-the-world," as Ralph Waldo Emerson later called it in his 1837 poem, *Concord Hymn.* That famous incident on the village green at Lexington, Massachusetts, and the running skirmish that followed along the road from Concord back to Lexington occurred on April 19, 1775. In that confrontation, local militia known as Minutemen mustered from their nearby homes into armed action against British soldiers who had come to take control of the gunpowder stored in the local armory.

Five-and-a-half years later and 800 miles from the site of that historic skirmish, another group of Patriot militiamen mustered in North Carolina to create some history of their own. These Southern Whig rebels were also fighting for the "common cause" of Liberty. The Overmountain Men of 1780, as they would thereafter be known, gathered from the hills and valleys of western North Carolina (including today's northeast Tennessee) and from the Holston Valley of southwest Virginia. They joined forces with Patriot militiamen from the Yadkin River valley, from the Piedmont of North Carolina, from South Carolina's Upcountry, and even a few from Georgia's backcountry. Together, they intended to confront an invading army fighting for the King. During two weeks, these Southern, backcountry militiamen crossed the Ap-

The Overmountain Victory, 1780

palachian mountain barrier and tracked down the western flank of Lord Cornwallis's advancing British Legion. After an all-night ride through a cold, rainy, October darkness, these Patriot militiamen surrounded their Loyalist quarry atop Little King's Mountain. In one hour on Octoboer 7, 1780, this determined host of Patriot militiaman won a decisive victory that helped turn the fortunes of the American Revolution. That fierce confrontation in the Carolina Piedmont became known as the Battle of Kings Mountain.

The War Moves South

During the first five years of fighting in the American Revolution (1775-1783), most of the battles occurred in the northern and mid-Atlantic states. The American Continental Army led by General George Washington had won a few battles and

the red-coated British Army had won a few; but, neither side was really winning the war. Neither had the Patriots won over all the colonists to their revolutionary cause. Only about one-third of the colonists supported the rebellion. A like number still supported the King. And, the rest were waiting to see which side was going to win before declaring their support. In the face of this lingering military stalemate and after capturing Savannah in late 1778, Sir Henry Clinton, the recently arrived British commander in the American Colonies, decided to renew the British "Southern Strategy." The British ministers and military leaders believed that the Southern colonies were filled with men who would fight for the Crown and against the Whig rebels. This revolution was, after all, challenging the King's sovereignty in the American colonies and threatening these Loyalists' rights as Englishmen. Those Americans who disliked radical change and preferred the status quo sided with the King.

On the day after Christmas 1779, General Clinton sailed from New York with his army. His British Legion force was composed mostly of American Loyalists, men from Connecticut, New York, New Jersey, and Pennsylvania. They arrived off the coast of South Carolina in the late winter of 1780. They began a siege of Charlestown on April 1. After General Benjamin Lincoln surrendered the city and his Southern Department of the Continental Army on May 12, General Clinton ordered his second-in-command, General Lord Charles Cornwallis, to march his army inland through the Carolinas and on to Virginia. Clinton also created a new position in charge of rallying and training the Southern Loyalists he expected to find in the Southern backcountry. He called it Inspector of Militia for the Carolinas and Georgia. He assigned an experienced and able officer to that post—a Scotsman, Major Patrick Ferguson.

During Cornwallis's advance through the center of South Carolina, Major Patrick Ferguson protected Cornwallis's left flank to the west. Ferguson was a soldier's soldier. He was an experienced field officer and was generally regarded as the best marksman in the British Army. Through his own personal grit and determination, he had overcome a severe injury to remain a reliable field commander. Committed and disciplined, Ferguson was having great success in recruiting citizens in the backcountry of South Carolina to join his army as Loyalists. The new recruits received British-made Brown Bess muskets and were trained how to fight with bayonets. None of the new recruits received British uniforms, however. They wore instead their everyday civilian clothes. When in battle against Patriot civilian partisans, also dressed as civilians, the Loyalists put sprigs of evergreen in their hats; Patriots tucked pieces of white paper in theirs, as they did at the battle of Ramsaur's Mill.

North Carolina Responds

Soon after the Southern Department of the Continental Army surrendered at Charlestown, Cornwallis's army began moving north toward the small community of Charlotte Town. Major Patrick Ferguson marched up the Wateree and Congaree rivers, forded the Saluda River, and marched into Ninety Six. From there he swept through the headwaters of western South Carolina successfully recruiting local citizens still loyal to the Crown to serve in the British ranks as armed Loyalists. During his advance, Ferguson's Loyalists were harassed by North Carolina militia from the Overmountain region and under the command of Colonel Isaac Shelby. They were joined by backcountry Georgia militia under Colonel Elijah Clarke. All these backwoods Patriots fought "Indian style," striking from cover with war whoops and yells. They attacked from ambush and then retreated, forcing the British to pursue them into the woods in a running skirmish.

In mid-August 1780, immediately after the Patriot victory at Musgrove's Mill, Major Ferguson's troops pursued the retreating rebel fighters, chasing Shelby's and Clarke's men northward into North Carolina as far at Gilbert Town. The Loyalists stopped their pursuit, however, enabling Shelby's men to escape back to the Overmountain region. Clarke's men rode back to Georgia.

The British Legion looked unstoppable. Lord Cornwallis had just defeated the Continental Army at Camden on August 16, a complete rout of the Southern Department's Patriot army that watched its leader, General Horatio Gates, abandon his men on the field of battle and ride away in fear for his life. The following month, on September 12, Colonel Charles McDowell, acting-commander of the North Carolina militia for the western district after

Colonel Charles McDowell ambushed Ferguson's force on September 12, 1780, near the upper ford on Cane Creek and then retreated to the Overmountain region. A marker stands along US Hwy 64 in Rutherford Co., NC, near the McDowell County line.

the capture of General Griffith Rutherford at Camden, ambushed Ferguson's patrol along Cane Creek. As was their practice as guerilla fighters, McDowell's men from Burke County attacked and retreated. They escaped to the far west, over the Blue Ridge and Appalachian mountains reaching the safety of the secluded Overmountain region in the valley of the Watauga River.

The Threat

From Gilbert Town, an irritated and frustrated Patrick Ferguson sent a message to the wily Overmountain Men using as his messenger a captured Patriot militiaman he released. When the messenger arrived in the Overmountain region of North Carolina, he re-

Isaac Shelby lived at Sapling Grove, the site of his father's fortified home. A marker stands at the site of Shelby's Fort on Anderson Street at 7th Street in Bristol, Tennessee. Another historical marker is mounted on a building wall two blocks north on 7th Street.

peated Ferguson's arrogant message to Isaac Shelby: "If you do not desist your opposition to the British Arms, I shall march this army over the mountains, hang your leaders, and lay your country waste with fire and sword."

Colonel Isaac Shelby wasted no time after hearing Ferguson's threat to march into their community, to terrorize them, and to destroy their homes. He saddled his horse and rode quickly from his home, Sapling Grove, in today's Bristol, Tennessee, forty miles to the home of Colonel John Sevier, another prominent militia leader in the Overmountain region. After careful consideration, the militia leaders decided it would be best if they crossed

From the Muster Grounds on Wolf Creek, 200 men marched to Sycamore Shoals to join their leader, Colonel William Campbell. The W. Blair Keller Visitor Center at the Muster Grounds is adjacent to the site at 702 Colonial Road, Abingdon, VA. This site is a trailhead of the Overmountain Victory National Historic Trail.

the mountains on their own terms and defeated Ferguson on the east side of the mountains. Thus did the would-be hunter become the hunted.

The Muster

The two Patriot leaders called for a mustering of militia units from throughout the Overmountain region and beyond. They sent express riders north and east calling

Mary Patton manufactured gunpowder for the Overmountain Men. The grave of Mary Patton is in the Patton-Simmons Cemetery on Toll Branch Road in northwest Carter County, Tennessee about two miles south of Milligan College.

upon Colonel Arthur Campbell and Colonel William Campbell to muster Virginians from the Holston River valley and the New River valley. They asked Colonel Benjamin Cleaveland and Major Joseph Winston to muster men from the Yadkin Valley in Wilkes and Surry counties in North Carolina and to meet them at Quaker Meadows. These Overmountain leaders called for a muster on September 25 at Sycamore Shoals, in the meadows surrounding Fort Watauga in today's Elizabethton, Tennessee.

The Overmountain Victory, 1780

Shelby brought 240 militiamen; Sevier brought a like number. William Campbell arrived from Abingdon in Washington County with 400 Virginians, half from his cousin's command. One hundred-sixty men from Burke County, under the command of Colonel McDowell, had taken refuge in the Overmountain region after their earlier skirmishes with Ferguson. Growing day by day to some one thousand strong in number, the militiamen prepared to cross the mountains, committed in their pursuit of the man who had threatened to invade their homeland: Major Patrick Ferguson.

While the militiamen waited for all to arrive, they prepared themselves for the cross-country campaign and the battle they expected to find at the end of it. Many of the men arrived with their families, who helped prepare the militiamen for their expedition. They tended their horses, saddles and tack, mended clothing and equipment, and prepared food such as parched corn and beef jerky. The men cleaned their long rifles and mined lead from the hillsides for making shot. While at Sycamore Shoals and in support of their fight for Liberty, they received 500 pounds of gunpowder from Mary Patton, a local powder maker.

The militiamen gathered along the Watauga River at Sycamore Shoals, interpreted today at Sycamore Shoals State Historic Area in Elizabethton, Tennessee on TN Hwy 67/US Hwy 321.

The Departure

On September 26, the throng of a thousand militiamen headed south from Sycamore Shoals, moving upstream along Gap Creek. Many of the men were on horseback, but others walked. This was not an army in the strictest sense of the word. All the men were civilians; none was a Continental soldier, though most were experienced militiamen, having fought for years against Cherokees, Chickamaugas, Shawnees, and tories. Some were fulfilling their service as militia; others volunteered for this campaign. Most expected to serve for only a few weeks before returning to their homes to tend to chores and personal matters. The militia did not follow strict military protocol. They elected their commanders, deciding among themselves

At the "Resting Place" on Doe River, the militiamen camped their first night of the march, storing their powder under a rock overhang to keep it dry in a light rain. Shelving Rock is on TN Hwy 143 between US Hwy 19E and Roan Mountain State Park.

whose leadership they would follow. The men were all skilled hunters and woodsmen. They were fighters, too, but they lacked the strict discipline of a military unit. For this last reason alone, the British military, regarded as the best army in the world, dismissed as irrelevant the threat from a fighting force composed of militia. Neither did the British officers think highly of the militia they were recruiting themselves. Nevertheless, Patrick Ferguson hoped to disprove this skepticism and to prove himself capable of preparing civilians to fight effectively.

On the night of the first day's march, the Patriot militiamen approached the foot of the mountains and camped along Doe River near today's Roan Mountain State Park in Tennessee. A light rain began to fall. To keep their gun powder dry, the men stored it under a rock overhang known today as Shelving Rock.

The Ascent

On the morning of the 27th, the militiamen began to ascend the Appalachian Mountain barrier. They followed Bright's Trace, which later became known as Yellow Mountain Road. It was little more than a horse path—most probably a buffalo trace later adopted by Indians as a footpath through the mountains. The militiamen followed it through the woods, ascending the steep slopes, riding and walking their horses as necessary up the difficult grade to reach the gap in the mountain ridge.

When the militiamen arrived at the saddle in the ridge at Yellow Mountain Gap, they found themselves in a

As the militiamen ascended Yellow Mountain, they could see behind them the valleys of their homesteads. A certified portion of the OVNH Trail in Tennessee climbs from Hampton Creek Cove to Yellow Mountain Gap.

The Overmountain Victory, 1780

meadow standing in snow that was recalled as "shoe mouth deep." The officers paraded the men and took a head count. They discovered that two of Sevier's men were missing: James Crawford and Samuel Chambers. The loyalty of these men to King George III was suspected by most. Some feared the two had deserted the campaign so they could run ahead and warn Major Ferguson that a host of Patriot militiamen was coming over the mountains to destroy his army of Loyalists. The militiamen had no choice but to continue their march. They descended the mountain a short distance and made camp along Roaring Creek.

On the 28th, the men proceeded along the plateau of the Blue Ridge following the North Toe River reaching by day's end Grassy Creek near today's Spruce Pine. Along the way, they passed Davenport Springs. The militiamen camped that night having covered 20 miles that day. On the next day, the men moved up Grassy Creek to Gillespie Gap along the edge of the Blue Ridge. From there they could see the Catawba Valley opening up before them. Knowing that two good paths descended the face of the mountains, the leaders were forced to make a bold decision. They split their force— a risky military move—so they could assure themselves that while they descended one path, Ferguson and his army of Loyalists were not coming up the other path. If Ferguson did, he and his army could have destroyed the militia-

men's home communities without any resistance. As it was, these militiamen were concerned as much that in their absence Dragging Canoe and his renegade Chickamaugas would attack their families. These militiamen wanted to find Ferguson, to deal with him quickly, and to return home as soon as possible.

The Gathering

Colonels Shelby and Sevier descended the mountains through Hefner Gap. Nearby McKinney Gap and Historic Orchard at Altapass are visible from Blue Ridge Parkway, MP 328. The nonprofit Altapass Foundation owns The Orchard and interprets the OVNH Trail.

The two parts of the divided force descended the face of the Blue Ridge into the valley of the North Fork Catawba River. The men under colonels Shelby and Sevier backtracked along the North Toe River to Hefner Gap, descending into the valley and camping near the mouth of Hunnycut's Creek at today's North Cove. Campbell's men took a more southerly route, descending to Turkey Cove along Armstrong Creek where they camped. The two parties advanced along separate routes the following day and re-united along the Catawba River just below today's Lake James. They arrived on the evening of the 30th at Quaker Meadows (in today's Morganton) and received the hospitality of brothers Colonel Charles McDowell and Major Joseph McDowell. The spirits of the militiamen were further lifted in camp on the 30th, when 350 militiamen under Colonel Cleaveland and Major Winston arrived following their four-day journey up the Yadkin River Valley from the mustering ground at Elkin

The Overmountain Men and the Yadkin River valley militia met at Quaker Meadows, the homes of Charles McDowell and Joseph McDowell. Owned by Historic Burke Foundation, the 1812 Charles McDowell home stands today off NC Hwy 181 on Saint Marys Church Rd. in Morganton, NC. Nothing remains of the 1780 home.

The Overmountain Victory, 1780

Major Joseph Winston mustered his Surry County militia at Elkin Creek and departed on Sept. 27, marching up the Yadkin River. Wayside exhibits overlooking the Mustering Ground (now Elkin City Park on NC Hwy 268) in Elkin, NC mark the trailhead of the eastern leg of the Overmountain Victory National Historic Trail.

Creek in today's Elkin, North Carolina.

Winston's and Cleaveland's militiamen from Surry County and Wilkes County had marched along the Yadkin River, camping near the Tory Oak, where Cleaveland often dispensed his brand of frontier justice by hanging tories. They rode on to the mouth of Elk Creek (near today's Ferguson, North Carolina), where they camped the second night, before passing by the fortified home of one of their own, Captain William Lenoir, at Fort Defiance on the third day. Receiving word by express rider from McDowell, they hurried on toward Quaker Meadows. They pressed on, leaving the headwaters of the Yadkin River, and crossed into the Catawba River basin where they camped on September 29 around Fort Crider. (The site is in today's Lenoir, North Carolina, a community known at the time as Tucker's Barn.) On the 30th, they forded the Johns River, and arrived to the hearty welcome of the men gathered under Shelby, Sevier, Campbell, and McDowell. To discuss their plans, the officers held a council of war in Quaker Meadows beneath the spreading branches of what became known as the Council Oak.

The party of Patriots headed south on October 1, traveling by a better road than had greeted them during the days before. They made better time for half a day until rain encouraged them to make camp at Bedford Hill, near the head of Cane Creek. On October 2, the rain continued and the men remained in camp for the day. No man had a tent. "Making camp" consisted of standing beneath the canopy of a tree,

At Quaker Meadows, the militia leaders met under a spreading oak tree, thereafter called the Council Oak. That tree and the gathering beneath it are commemorated by a monument on NC Hwy 181 at Bost Rd. in Morganton, NC.

the leaves of which were beginning to turn red and yellow and to fall to the ground. Or perhaps some built a lean-to; no doubt they struggled to keep fires burning. As these militiamen were not highly disciplined troops, fights broke out among the men, or nearly so, as their patience was wearing thin. They had been on the trail for a week and were becoming increasingly anxious about the welfare of their families back across the mountains. They were ready to find Ferguson.

The militia officers met that night in camp at Bedford Hill to consider how best to proceed. They had information that Ferguson was nearby at Gilbert Town. As they prepared to go into battle, they agreed they would need a general commander. Colonel McDowell volunteered to ride off to Hillsboro to see if General Gates would assign a Continental officer to lead them. Colonel Shelby would have none of that delay. He suggested that as Colonel Campbell had brought the most men and had come the farthest, he should take command of the expedition. Shelby also knew that because all the colonels there were from North Carolina except Campbell, some jealousy might arise if one of the others were selected. Shelby's plan prevailed and William Campbell became the general commander of the expedition.

On the morning of October 3, before the men were to continue the march, colonels Cleveland and Shelby called all the men together to address them. The two colonels encouraged the men and gave them all one last chance to back out of the coming confrontation. To drop out of the fight, they had only to take three steps to the rear. Not a single man shirked his duty. The gathering of Patriot mili-

tiamen cheered their own bravery and their commitment to the cause.

Shelby continued, "I am heartily glad to see you to a man resolve to meet and fight your country's foes. When we encounter the enemy, don't

The militiamen camping at Bedford Hill, on a "breakwater" dividing the Catawba and Broad river basins, may have spread across the area drawing water from Magazine Creek and Cane Creek. Looking north from FortuneRoad on Bedford Hill across Magazine Creek toward Pilot Mountain (in photo), one can see the South Mountains to the east and the gap through which the militiamen rode (right center of photo) where today's US Hwy 64 passes.

The Overmountain Victory, 1780

wait for the word of command. Let each one of you be your own officer, and do the very best you can, taking every care you can of yourselves and availing yourselves of every advantage that chance may throw in your way. If in the woods, shelter yourselves, and give them Indian play; advance from tree to tree, pressing the enemy and killing and disabling all you can."

The Patriot forces descended Cane Creek, passing the log building Brittain Church, erected in 1768. New Brittain Church and cemetery are on US Hwy 64 seven miles north of Rutherfordton, NC.

Shelby dismissed the men who busied themselves preparing for the march. They were told to make two meals for their wallets and haversacks. When done, they received a ration of liquor promised them by Colonel Cleaveland and Major Joseph McDowell. The men took up the march for a few miles following Cane Creek and then camped for the night beneath the presence of Marlin's Knob.

On the morning of October 4, the men continued their march toward Gilbert Town where they expected to find Ferguson encamped. The march was slow as the path crossed and re-crossed Cane Creek many times. As the Overmountain Men approached Gilbert Town, they passed by Brittain Church. Along the way, they also learned from a local Patriot that Ferguson had already departed.

The Search

Indeed, on the evening of September 30 as the Patriot forces were gathering at Quaker Meadows, the two deserters, Crawford and Chambers,

Gilbert Town, established in 1779 in Rutherford County, was occupied at different times by both Patriot militia and Ferguson's Loyalist forces. The site of the former Gilbert Town lies two or three miles northeast of Rutherfordton, North Carolina on Rock Rd. about 600 feet northeast of Old Gilbertown Road.

had arrived at the Loyalist camp. They had told Ferguson about the Overmountain Men crossing the mountains to pursue him. Ferguson immediately recognized his predicament. He had furloughed some of his Loyalist recruits so they could visit home and tend to personal matters. Ferguson realized he now needed to gather his men quickly and to retreat toward Charlotte Town where Cornwallis's larger army was encamped. Ferguson also realized he needed even more recruits than he had, so he immediately issued an appeal for more citizens in the surrounding vicinity to join his army: "Unless you wish to be eat up by an inundation of barbarians ... grasp your arms in a moment and run to camp ... The Back Water men have crossed the mountains ... If you choose to be degraded forever and ever by a set of mongrels, say so at once, and let your women turn their backs upon you, and look out for real men to protect them. – Pat. Ferguson, Major 71st Regiment."

Ferguson marched his men toward Charlotte Town but took some evasive action and actually remained in one camp for two days awaiting word from his scouts on the whereabouts of his pursuers. On October 6, Ferguson sent a message to General Cornwallis advising his plans and asking for reinforcements. He wrote in part, "I am on my march towards you, by a road leading from Cherokee Ford, north of King's Mountain. Three or four hundred good soldiers, part dragoons, would finish the business. Something must be done soon. This is their last push in the quarter, etc. – Patrick Ferguson."

The assemblage of Overmountain Men and backcountry Patriots continued their pursuit of Major Ferguson. They suspected he might be moving to the southwest and retreating to the safety of the Loyalist regiments at Ninety Six. The Patriots followed that path until the evening of October 5, when Colonel Edward Lacey rode into their camp at the ford on Green River to advise them that Ferguson was headed toward Charlotte Town. Lacey, a Patriot and a colonel of the South Carolina partisans, was not known to the leaders of the Overmountain Men. They were suspicious of his information and motives. But finally convinced by his earnestness and demeanor that he was reliable, the Patriot force abruptly changed its direction. The leaders divided their forces into mounted and footmen. The mounted militia rode hard all day October 6 to reach The Cowpens. They were followed hours later by the equally earnest footmen. Colonel Lacey and Colonel William Hill joined them there with their band of partisans from South Carolina, men who had been mustered and trained by Colonel Thomas Sumter, although Sumter was not then commanding them. Some thirty Georgians, part of Colonel Elijah Clarke's militia unit, had joined the Patriots as well, near the ford on Green River. The entire party of Patriots then numbered over 2,000; still, none among them was a Continental soldier or officer.

The Pursuit

Scouts soon reported to the Patriots the movements of Ferguson and his Loyalists. Learning that Ferguson was so near the safety of Charlotte Town, the Patriots knew they had only one day to overtake him. They had to move more quickly than an outfit of their number could maneuver. The leaders formed a smaller group of about half their number, choosing from their ranks the 910 best marksmen mounted on the 910 best horses. At about nine o'clock, the chosen militiamen rode out from The Cowpens into a cold October night. Rain began to fall. The men took off their hunting frocks and wrapped them around their powder and their rifles, to keep them dry and ready to fire. Though the men had already covered 21 miles that day and had been in the saddle for two weeks pursuing Patrick Ferguson, they now had to cover 35 miles more through an all-night ride to overtake their quarry. The rain and the dark confused some members of the party who took a wrong turn. They nevertheless slogged along muddy roads through a long and tiring night. At mid-morning, they reached the Cherokee Ford over the Broad River. Though the day was cool and the river was swelling from the recent rains, the men and their horses crossed without incident. The militiamen on the sturdiest horses crossed first and braced them against the current so the others could pass. The skies began to clear. The warming sun dried out the saddle-weary riders and lifted their spirits. Those who had failed to get a meal at The Cowpens stripped green corn from the fields they passed. They and their horses were tiring, but they remained fixed on one goal: they had only to find their prey.

Riding and marching hard all day October 6, the mounted and foot militia arrived at The Cowpens to join with the South Carolina militia. A segment of the old road into Cowpens National Battlefield is the route followed by the Patriot militia coming from the Green River ford.

The mounted Patriot militia rode through a cold, rainy night, crossing the Broad River at Cherokee Ford where some of them had encamped earlier under Colonel McDowell. Cherokee Ford is about 1.5 miles south of US Hwy 29 off SC Hwy 239 and off Ford Road.

As the Patriots continued riding east, they learned from local residents that Ferguson was encamped atop Little King's Mountain, an area known well to one of the militia officers who had joined them from Lincoln County. It was a promontory rising about 60 feet above the surrounding terrain. The top was about 600 yards long and tapering from 120 yards wide to 60 yards. The sides were covered with trees and rocks. As the Patriot force of nine hundred-and-some mounted militiamen rode toward the mountain, the wet trail prevented any tell-tale dust from rising up to spoil their surprise attack.

Ferguson had selected his campsite on top of the mountain believing that the high ground afforded him a military advantage should the Patriot militia catch up to him. He was later reported as having declared "he was on King's Mountain, that he was king of that mountain and God Almighty could not drive him from it." His confidence in this strategy was soon tested.

The militiamen stopped in the woods, dismounted, and tied their horses, leaving behind their blankets and hunting frocks and everything except what they would need in battle: their rifles, their shot and their powder, their tomahawks, and their hunting knives. The Patriot leaders divided the men into two columns. They were to advance separately until they surrounded the mountain and then advance up the sides simultaneously from all directions. Final orders were given the men: "Fresh prime in your guns, and every man go into battle firmly resolving to fight till he dies."

The Overmountain Victory, 1780

The war and the world were about to change.
It was Saturday, October 7,
three o'clock in the afternoon.

The Battle

The militiamen proceeded quickly to surround the mountain and were within a quarter-mile of the camp before sentries first spied the advancing force. The Patriot militia continued to encircle the mountain as Ferguson, alerted to their presence, mounted his horse and signaled orders to his men with trills from his silver whistle.

Though most of Ferguson's men, and certainly his recent recruits, wore their civilian clothes, a few units of British Legion Loyalists did wear red-coat uniforms. These rangers were the units that first encountered the attacking Patriots. Shelby's men met them in the woods and gave

On the evening of October 6, Major Patrick Ferguson set his camp atop Little King's Mountain. The US Monument at Kings Mountain National Military Park stands at the site of Ferguson's camp where the closing events of the battle occurred.

them "Indian play," firing from behind trees and rocks which sheltered them from the musket fire of the Loyalists. Other units of Patriots were also advancing up the faces of King's Mountain and encountering the same resistance organized by Ferguson. Fortunately for the militiamen, the Loyalists shooting downhill with their Brown Bess muskets tended to shoot high and over the heads of the Patriots. Unfortunately, the Loyalists also had bayonets and upon Ferguson's orders, the Loyalists advanced downhill with bayonets fixed in an organized attack. To the Patriot militiamen, it was a fearsome sight. The militiamen, needing a full minute to reload their long rifles, had no choice but to retreat in the face of a bayonet charge. When the Loyalists reached the bottom of the hill, they stopped pursuing the Patriots and returned to the top.

To their credit, the Patriot militia did not accept their momentary retreat as defeat. All around the mountain, the Patriot militiamen, once repelled by bayonet charges, remounted their attack. Again they advanced up the faces of the mountain, taking deadly aim with their hunting rifles and claiming victim after victim. The Loyalists forced the Patriot militiamen back down the mountain at the point of bayonets a second time. And again, from the bottom of the hill, the militiamen remounted their attack. On their third assault, the Patriots took the crest of King's Mountain.

By this time, the side of the mountain was covered in a sulfurous haze of gunpowder smoke issued from 2,000 muskets and rifles fired repeatedly during an hour-long battle. The Patriots pressed forward, encircling the Loyalists at the northeast end of the promontory. Ferguson, sensing defeat and knowing that he was about to be captured, rode hurriedly toward the Patriot line expecting to escape by charging through the militiamen. Robert Young, a 62-year old North Carolina militiaman from today's Johnson City, Tennessee, took aim with his

The body of Major Patrick Ferguson was wrapped in a raw cow hide and buried with the body of Virginia Sal, one of his cooks and a supposed mistress. A marker placed in 1930, on the 150th anniversary, stands at Ferguson's traditional Scottish burial cairn. It was placed by US citizens to recognize friendship with British citizens.

The Overmountain Victory, 1780

rifle and shot Ferguson out of his saddle. Ferguson's foot caught in the stirrup and as the horse dragged the body of the despised British officer around the mountain top, at least six other Patriot militiamen fired into the body. Many more later claimed to have done so.

With Ferguson dead, the Loyalist resistance quickly evaporated. Loyalitst Captain Abraham DePeyster, second in command, ordered his troops to surrender. Chaos and confusion reigned over the next several minutes. Recalling the slaughter of Colonel Abraham Buford's Continentals at the hands of Lt. Colonel Banastre Tarleton on May 29 in the Waxhaws, the militiamen fired into the ranks of surrendering Loyalists, shouting "Give them Buford's quarter." William Campbell rushed forward and struggled to regain control of the situation. In the melee, someone fired at Colonel James Williams, mortally wounding the South Carolina militia leader. With the firing finally stopped, the Loyalists stacked their weapons and became prisoners of the Patriots. Through the remainder of the afternoon and evening, the men on both sides tended to some of their wounded and buried their dead in shallow graves, covering some bodies with only logs and rocks. The Patriots dared not linger long as they feared that Tarleton's dragoons might appear at any moment. Unwilling to burden themselves with the captured supplies, the Patriots burned the wagons on top of the mountain.

The remains of Colonel James Williams were moved and reinterred in Gaffney, South Carolina. The grave and markers are at 210 N. Limestone Street (SC Hwy 150) at the Cherokee County administration offices.

The Withdrawal

On the morning of October 8th, the Patriots departed King's Mountain with about 800 prisoners. Each Loyalist prisoner carried a weapon or two, disabled by removing the flint. The victorious Patriot militiamen with their prisoners made their way back toward Gilbert Town. Colonel Williams succumbed to his wounds by noon and was buried that night at their campsite. A week later, as the militiamen marched their prisoners northward, they demanded retribution against some of the Loyalists they had captured. The militiamen claimed that some were guilty of atrocities against the Patriots and their kin. On October 14, the militiamen held

In camp at Biggerstaff's farm in eastern Rutherford County, the withdrawing Patriot militiamen tried 32 Tory prisoners and hanged nine of them, including Colonel Ambrose Mills. The marker is west of Sunshine on Green Street, about ten miles northeast of Bypass US Hwy 74 in Ruth (adjacent to Rutherfordton), North Carolina.

quick trials and condemned 32 of the men to death. Nine were hanged from a tree at the Biggerstaff plantation before Colonel Shelby stopped the slaughter. Receiving a rumor that Tarleton's dragoons were close on their heels, the Patriots departed quickly on the morning of October 15, pressing on through a hard rain and along muddy roads, and fording the Catawba River just before they would have been trapped on the south side by the rain-swollen river.

Over the next several days, some of the Patriot militiamen disbanded, returning to their respective homes. Colonel John Sevier and many of the Overmountain Men re-crossed the Appalachian Mountains. Among them was Robert Sevier, nursing a serious wound and traveling with a nephew. Nine days after the battle, he stopped at Davenport Springs and while there, in a matter of minutes, succumbed to his injury and died. The nephew buried Sevier near the spring.

Captain Robert Sevier succumbed to a mortal wound on his way home, nine days after the battle.

At Quaker Meadows, Colonel William Campbell and Colonel Isaac Shelby took charge of the prisoners. With Colonel Benjamin Cleveland of Wilkes County and Major Joseph Winston of Surry County, they rode down the Yadkin River valley toward the succor and safety of the Moravian towns, Bethania and Bethabara. Two weeks after the battle, the Patriots and their prisoners descended upon the unsuspecting Moravians, who, as was their practice, took care of the wounded, the hungry, and those in need. The demands placed on the Moravian villagers left them little if anything for themselves. The army lingered for 19 days, and although the prisoners were kept in a stockade, many of the Loyalists escaped. After nearly three weeks, the Patriots marched the remaining prisoners off toward Hillsborough. The Moravians wrote, "It gave us much pleasure to see the soldiers march away, though we were very sorry for the poor men who are in great need."

Epilogue

Word of Ferguson's death and the total defeat of his Loyalists at King's Mountain surprised and disheartened General Lord Charles Cornwallis. With the losses of his army's western flank and one of his most talented officers, Cornwallis could no longer proceed confidently with his planned advance northward from Charlotte Town into North Carolina. Falling seriously ill himself and with his army in some disarray, Cornwallis and his British Legion retreated with difficulty to Winnsborough, South Carolina for a winter camp.

The Patriot victory at King's Mountain had other effects as well. No longer could the British depend on American Loyalists in the Carolina Piedmont to flock eagerly to their standard. The Patriot spirit was reinvigorated and the British Southern campaign had been dealt a substantial blow. Though additional victories on other Carolina battlefields (e.g., Cowpens and Guilford Courthouse) would be required to secure America's independence, the battle at King's Mountain was a major turning point in the American Revolution. Forty-two years later, Thomas Jefferson would recall that battle as "the joyful annunciation of

General Lord Cornwallis's British Army was trapped on the peninsula at Yorktown by General George Washington with a Patriot force joined by the French Army and French Navy. The Victory Monument at Yorktown, VA commemorates the British surrender on October 19, 1781.

that turn of the tide of success which terminated the Revolutionary War wit the seal of our independence." Indeed, General George Washington's Continental Army had been fighting for five-and-half years without decisive effect. His strategy had been to thwart the British simply by keeping an army in the field; yet, only 12 months and 12 days after the Battle of Kings Mountain, General Lord Charles Cornwallis surrendered his British Army at Yorktown. The American Revolution had succeeded, and a new country was free to pursue its own destiny with Liberty.

Planning Your Visit to the OVNHT

The Overmountain Victory National Historic Trail (OVNHT) is 330 miles long and runs through four states. Planning your visit will enhance your experience of the Trail. It is larger and longer than can be properly experienced in a day or even a weekend. Opportunities abound along the Trail for touring museums and visitor centers, learning the history, strolling or biking along segments of the Trail, hiking more challenging Trail segments, photographing vistas and monuments, and taking side trips to points of related interest along the Trail.

The OVNHT is not a cross-country hiking route. The following itinerary is intended to help heritage tourists plan their visits to the various sites along the Trail by automobile. The following terms are used to suggest three types of driving that will be useful along the Trail.

Driving – getting from point to point directly and expeditiously
Touring – getting around to separate local points in a common, general location
Visiting – engaging in learning through available media and activities, most often out of the automobile, e.g., museums, hikes, vistas, exhibits, monuments, markers

Map Panel # 1 – Abingdon to Choate's Ford

Campbell's Grave

From Abingdon, VA, 25 miles. Allow 1.5 – 2 hrs for driving, touring, visit, and return. No services.

Muster Grounds and surrounding markers

In Abingdon, allow 1-1.5 hrs for touring and visits. Markers. Waysides. Museum exhibits. Bookstore. Restrooms. Walking trail.

(Other sites in Abingdon are of historical interest for this era. See Abingdon Visitor Center at 335 Cummings Street, one half mile off I-81, Exit 17. Also, www.abingdon.com)

Pemberton Oak

From Abingdon, VA, 14 miles. Allow 40-50 minutes for driving and visit. Remnant tree trunk. Private property. Viewing from road and from outside the fence is allowed. Historical markers.

Choate's Ford and surrounding markers

From Pemberton Oak, 16 miles. Allow 45-60 minutes for driving, touring and visits. Markers. Waysides. Water feature. Informational kiosk. Walking trail.

Side trip to Bristol

From Pemberton Oak, 10 miles. Allow 45-60 minutes for driving, touring, and visits. Markers and plaques.

Choate's Ford from Bristol: 11 miles via US Hwy 11W/19; 13 miles via US Hwy 421 and TN Hwy 394.

Map Panel # 2 – Choate's Ford to Gap Creek

Rocky Mount Museum State Historic Site (admission fee)

From Choate's Ford (Bluff City, TN), 7 miles. Allow 1.5 - 2 hours or more for driving and visit. Restrooms. Gift/Book shop. Museum. Movie. Guided tour. Living history interpreters. (www.rockymountmuseum.com)

Side trip to Robert Young Cabin

From Rocky Mount Museum State Historic Site, 1.8 miles south on US Hwy 11W/19. See refurbished and relocated cabin of man who is credited with shooting Major Patrick Ferguson at King's Mountain. Allow 20 - 30 minutes for touring and visit.

Sycamore Shoals State Historic Area

From Rocky Mount Museum State Historic Site, 16 miles. Allow 1.5 -2 hours or more for driving, touring, and visit. Museum. Trail. Replica fort. Markers and monuments. Movie. Bookstore. Restrooms. (*www.tn.gov/environment/parks/SycamoreShoals*)

Side trip to Carter Mansion

From Sycamore Shoals State Historic Area, 4 miles. Allow 1-1.5 hours for touring and visit. Arrange tour at visitor center for Sycamore Shoals SHA. House tour. Cemetery.

1013 Broad Street, 100 yards east of US Hwy 19E.

Side trip to Mary Patton's Grave
    From Sycamaore Shoals State Historic Area, follow US Hwy 321/TN 67 southwest for 2.0 miles to TN Hwy 359. Turn right for 1.9 miles to Milligan College. Drive 1/2 mile through campus on Milligan College Drive to Toll Branch Road. Turn left and proceed 1.5 miles to Patton-Simmons Cemetery on hilltop to left.

Gap Creek Monument

From Sycamore Shoals State Historic Area, 5 miles. Allow 15-20 minutes for driving and visit.

Map Panel # 3 – Gap Creek to Roaring Creek

Town of Roan Mountain

From Gap Creek monument, 15 miles. Allow 25 – 40 minutes for driving. Trail.

Shelving Rock (*Warning: It is unsafe to stop at this site.*)

From Town of Roan Mountain, 1.5 miles. Allow 5-10 minutes for drive-by look and return. No services.

Shelving Rock Encampment

From Shelving Rock, 200 yards south on TN Hwy 143. Allow 5 minutes for visit. Private property. Do not trespass. Land owner has erected an informational sign about the site at entrance.

Hampton Creek Cove State Natural Area

From Shelving Rock, about 4 miles. Hike is moderate to strenuous. Allow 3-4 hours for ascent and return. Take water and dress properly. No services. Appropriate only for the prepared.

Roaring Creek Road

From Town of Roan Mountain, 15 miles. Allow 30-40 minutes for driving. Follow US Hwy 19E east, turning right after Elk Park and continuing south on US Hwy 19E along winding road in some sections to reach Roaring Creek Road at the historical marker for "Yellow Mountain Road." Travelers may drive up Roaring Creek Road onto unpaved road and into US Forest Service land to end of road just below Yellow Mountain

Gap. Hike to Yellow Mountain Gap is moderate, but the route is not well marked. Take water and dress properly. No services. Appropriate only for the prepared. Allow 1.5-2 hours for touring, hiking, and return to US Hwy 19E.

Map Panel # 4 – Roaring Creek to North Cove and Turkey Cove

Davenport Springs

(Restricted Access) Davenport Springs is on private land to the east of US 19E northeast of Spruce Pine, NC. Access is limited to annual OVTA reenactment on September 28. Contact *www.OVTA.org*.

Robert Sevier Grave

(Restricted Access) Cemetery is on private land to the east of US 19E northeast of Spruce Pine, NC. Access is limited to annual OVTA reenactment on September 28. Contact *www.OVTA.org*.

Grassy Creek campsite

From Roaring Creek Road, 16 miles. Allow 30-40 minutes for driving and touring. See 1910 DAR marker near train depot on Locust Ave. in Spruce Pine, NC.

Gillespie Gap (Museum of North Carolina Minerals)

From Grassy Creek campsite, 6 miles. Allow 10 minutes for driving and 1 hour for visit. Mineral exhibits, OVNHT exhibit. Restrooms. NPS bookstore. Views to the east of the Catawba River valley are available from along NC Hwy 226A as far west as Little Switzerland. NC Hwy 226A should **not** be taken as a route down the mountain; it is too curvy, steep, and narrow.

The Loops Overlook (near McKinney Gap) and Hefner Gap

From Museum of North Carolina Minerals, 3 miles. Allow 10-15 minutes touring along Blue Ridge Parkway to The Loops Overlook at Mile Post 328. See North Fork Catawba River valley and McKinney Gap. The Historic Orchard at Altapass, owned by the non-profit Altapass Foundation, is immediately below the overlook. Open seasonally, Memorial Day Weekend into October. Interprets the OVNHT. Restrooms. Souvenir shopping. Books. Music. Hayrides. Storytelling. Apples. Allow 1-3 hours. (*www.altapassorchard.com*) Continue on Blue Ridge Parkway to Mile Post 326 for overlook at Hefner Gap, (spelled "Heffner" along BRP).

Turkey Cove encampment

(Unmarked site near intersection of Old NC Hwy 221 and American Thread Road)

From Museum of North Carolina Minerals, 8 miles. Allow 20-30 minutes driving. Descend steep, curving, east face of Blue Ridge Mountains on NC Hwy 226 to US Hwy 221. (**Warning: Drive cautiously and use lower gear; do not "ride" your brakes.**) Continue east as if NC 226 were extended to be on Old NC Hwy 221. Intersection at end of that road with American Thread Road is near confluence of Armstrong Creek and North Fork Catawba River, that is, Turkey Cove. Continue to North Cove or return to US Hwy 221.

North Cove encampment

(Unmarked site on North Cove School Road between US Hwy 221 and Old Linville Road.)

From intersection of Old US Hwy 221 and American Thread Road (i.e. Turkey Cove), 4 miles. Allow 10 minutes for drive-by tour of North Cove area. Trailhead of US Forest Service Trail #308 in the Pisgah Forest departs from Old Linville Road in North Cove. Hike is moderate to strenuous. Take water and dress properly. No services. Appropriate only for the prepared.

Map Panel # 5 – North Cove and Turkey Cove to Quaker Meadows

Joseph McDowell House in Marion

From North Cove/Turkey Cove, 6 miles. Allow 10 – 15 minutes for driving. House is 100 yards east of US Hwy 221 on US 70. House may be open seasonally with changing exhibits.

Side Trip to Historic Carson House

From US Hwy 221, go 2.7 miles west on US Hwy 70 to Pleasant Gardens. Allow 1 hour for touring and visit. House tour. Artifacts display and family research library. Donations welcomed. No services.(www.historiccarsonhouse.com)

Side Trip to Mountain Gateway Museum

From US Hwy 221, go 10.3 miles to Catawba Ave. in Old Fort, NC. Go ½ mile south. Also, from Exit 72 from I-40. A sister museum of the North Carolina Museum of History.

Quaker Meadows in Morganton

Charles McDowell House

Scenic route: From US Hwy 221 via US Hwy 70 and NC Hwy 126, 30 miles. Allow 50-60 minutes.

Fastest route: From US Hwy 221 via NC Hwy 226, I-40, US Hwy 64, Sanford Drive, and NC Hwy 181, 30 miles. Allow 35-40 minutes. Restrooms. House tour, Sundays 2-4, April – October. (*www.historicburke.org*)

Council Oak marker

From Charles McDowell House on St. Mary's Church Rd., ½ mile. Allow 10 minutes touring and visit. Marker. Marker is on NW corner of Green Street (NC Hwy 181) and Bost Road.

Quaker Meadows Cemetery

From Council Oak marker, 1 mile. Allow 10 minutes for touring and visit. Cemetery is gated. Admittance is by appointment only through Historic Burke Foundation.

OVNHT along the Catawba River Greenway

From Council Oak marker on N. Green Street (NC Hwy 181), 1 mile. Allow 1-3 hours for a walk or bike ride along OVNHT along the river. Accessible from commercial parking lot for River Village on the Greenway. Also accessible from Catawba Meadows Park on Sanford Drive about ½ mile north of NC Hwy 181 and from Rocky Ford access at US Hwy 64 at Catawba River. See "Map Panel #8 - Quaker Meadows to Gilbert Town" for additional access to OVNHT along Catawba River Greenway.

Map Panel #6 – Elkin Creek to Fort Defiance

Mustering Ground

Elkin City Park on US Hwy 268, 1.5 miles northwest of Elkin Town Hall. Wayside exhibits and historical marker overlooking park. Walking trail along Elkin Creek and Yadkin River. Allow 10 minutes for touring and visit to waysides. Allow 1.5 – 2 hours for walking along trail.

Benjamin Cleveland marker

From Elkin City Park, about 4 miles southwest along NC Hwy 268. Allow 10 minutes for driving and visit.

Wilkes Heritage Museum

From Benjamin Cleveland marker, about 16 miles. Allow 30-40 minutes driving. Museum in refurbished 1902 courthouse (admission charged). Restrooms. Bookstore. Gift shop. (*www.wilkesheritagemuseum.com*)

Tory Oak

Adjacent to Wilkes Heritage Museum on northeast corner of block. A certified site of the OVNHT. Wayside exhibit. Commemorative tree planting.

Robert Cleveland Log Cabin

One block to northwest of Wilkes Heritage Museum. Tours scheduled Tuesday - Saturday. Check with museum.

Yadkin River Greenway and OVNHT

Trailhead is adjacent to Robert Cleveland cabin. Descends steeply in ¼ mile to pedestrian bridge over Yadkin River and to Yadkin River Greenway. Allow 30 minutes to 2 hours or more for walk. No services. (*www.yadkinrivergreenway.com*)

Moravian Creek Access to Yadkin River Greenway

From Wilkes Heritage Museum, 1.7 miles. Allow 5 minutes for driving and 30 minutes to 2 hours for walk. No services.

W. Kerr Scott Reservoir Visitor Assistance Center

From Moravian Creek Access, 3 miles on NC Hwy 268 west. Allow 30-60 minutes for museum exhibits and views of lake and valley. Allow 1-3 hours for walking along OVNHTrail segment. Restrooms. Small bookstore. (*www.saw.usace.army.mil/wkscott*)

Fish Dam Creek Overlook and trailhead for OVNHT

From W. Kerr Scott Reservoir Visitor Assistance Center, ½ mile across top of dam. Allow 5-10 minutes for touring and viewing. Allow 1-2 hours for walking.

Mountain View Overlook

From W. Kerr Scott Reservoir Visitor Assistance Center, 6.5 miles. Allow 30-45 minutes for driving and observing views of Yadkin River valley to northeast and Blue Ridge Mountains to west.

Side trip to Whippoorwill Academy and Village
From W. Kerr Scott Reservoir Visitor Assistance Center, about nine miles on NC

Hwy 268 along the Yadkin River. Open May to October. Family farm with replica cabin of Daniel Boone's Beaver Creek homestead. Period buildings including jail and blacksmith shop. Canoe rentals (seasonally). Small bookstore, art display, and gift shop. A genuine, functioning outhouse is available. (See Whippoorwill Academy on Facebook.)

Fort Defiance

From Mountain View Overlook, 15 miles. Allow 1.5 – 2.5 hours for driving and visit to 1792 home of William Lenoir. Tour of grounds and home. Admission charged. Restrooms. Small book/gift shop. Open Thursday – Saturday 10-5, Sunday, 1-5. (*www.fortdefiancenc.org*)

Map Panel # 7 – Fort Defiance to Quaker Meadows

Yadkin River Greenway of Caldwell County

From Fort Defiance, 5 miles. Allow 1-2 hours for walk if desired. No services.

Fort Crider site

From Yadkin River Greenway of Caldwell County, 6 miles. Allow 30 minutes for driving and visiting marker in Lenoir at corner of Willow Street and Harper Ave.

Johns River Crossing

From Lenoir, 12 miles. Allow 30 minutes for driving. OVNHT crosses Johns River on US 64. Boat launch. No services.

Rocky Ford Access to Catawba River Greenway

From Johns River Crossing, 2.0 miles. Allow 5 minutes for driving. Allow 1-3 hours for walking, if desired. No services. Future site of OVNHT headquarters and visitor center.

Catawba Meadows Park Access to Catawba River Greenway

From Rocky Ford Access, 1.2 miles to park entrance on Sanford Drive (US Hwy 64 Truck). Allow 1-3 hours for walking, if desired. Restrooms. (*www.ci.morganton.nc.us/index.php/residents-menu/catawba-river-greenway*)

See "Map Panel # 5 – North Cove and Turkey Cove to Quaker Meadows" for additional sites on the OVNHT in Morganton.

Map Panel #8 – Quaker Meadows to Gilbert Town

Greenlee Ford Access to Catawba River Greenway

From intersection of Sanford Drive (US Hwy 64 Truck) and North Green St. (NC Hwy 181), 2 miles. Greenlee Ford Access is adjacent to Catawba River Soccer Complex on Greenlee Ford Road 0.2 miles off US Hwy 70 about 0.4 miles west of Sanford Dr. (US 64 Truck). Allow 5 minutes for driving and 1-3 hours for walking and bike riding if desired. Historic Greenlee Ford is observable in river. Restaurant adjacent. Commercial district nearby.

Pilot Mountain

From Greenlee Ford Access, 13 miles. Allow 20-30 minutes driving. View landscape from US Hwy 64 as it passes through gap.

Bedford Hill

From gap along US Hwy 64 at Pilot Mountain, 1.5 miles. Drive over Bedford Hill along Bill Deck Road, unpaved. Observe landscape. No markers.

Cane Creek historical marker

From Bedford Hill, 1.5 miles (0.9 miles south of NC Hwy 226 overpass). Allow 3 minutes for driving. **Unsafe to stop at marker.** Narrow shoulder next to busy highway. Cane Creek is observable adjacent to east side of US Hwy 64 of several miles. No services.

Marlin's Knob

From Cane Creek historical marker, 3 miles. Observe landscape from road. OVNHT follows Cane Creek Road for 6 miles to rejoin US Hwy 64. No services. (Cane Creek Mountain Road is **not** the same as Cane Creek Road.)

Brittain Church and Cemetery

From Marlin's Knob (i.e., US Hwy 64 at Cane Creek Road at north end), 6.5 miles. Allow 20-30 minutes for drive through picturesque, rural area.(From US Hwy 64 at Cane Creek Road at south end, ½ mile.) No services.

Gilbert Town Marker

From Brittain Church, 7 miles. Allow 20-30 minutes for touring and visiting markers.

Side trip to Rutherford County Office Building at 289 North Main Street. (Gilbert Town exhibits and artifacts displayed). Across the street is Historic St. John's Church, built 1849. From Gilbert Town marker, about 4 miles. Allow 45–60 minutes for touring and visit. Additional historic markers on courthouse lawn south of Rutherford County Office Building.

Biggerstaff's Old Fields

From Rutherfordton/Ruth, 10 miles. Allow 45-60 minutes to drive, visit marker, and return. (Have a good map with you.) Future exhibits are planned for site.

Map Panel #9 - Gilbert Town to The Cowpens

Alexander's Ford and Bradley Nature Preserve

From Rutherfordton/Ruth (US Hwy 74-Alt and Green Street), 8 miles. Allow 20-25 minutes for driving. This site is currently under development and not available for access.

Cowpens National Battlefield

From Rutherfordton (NC Hwy 108 at US Hwy Bus 74), 38 miles by way of Mill Spring. The OVNHT Motorized Route is the recommended route for traveling through this area unless travelers have a good map and a good sense of direction. Follow NC Hwy 108 southwest for 14 miles to Mill Spring at NC Hwy 9. Follow a series of state highways which change numbers across the North Carolina-South Carolina line (see text for Map Panel # 9) to reach Cowpens National Battlefield on SC Hwy 11 near intersection with US Hwy 221 Alt. (*www.nps.gov/cowp*)

Map Panel # 10 – The Cowpens to King's Mountain

Colonel James Williams's Grave

From Cowpens National Battlefield, 15 miles. Allow 30-45 minutes for driving, touring, and visiting. No services, but commercial district is nearby.

Cherokee Ford

From Gaffney, 7.5 miles. Allow 30 minutes for driving and visit. View of river. No markers. No services.

Kings Mountain National Military Park

From Cherokee Ford, 12 miles. Allow 30-40 minutes driving along back roads. Accessible from SC Hwy 216 off I-85 at Exit 2 in North Carolina. Allow 2-4 hours for movie, museum, and battlefield walking trail with monuments and wayside exhibits. Bookstore. Restrooms. (*www.nps.gov/kimo*)

If you have suggestions for improving the information provided here to help visitors get around to the sites along the Overmountain Victory National Historic Trail, please contact us with your feedback at *DBooneFootsteps@gmail.com.*

Notes

Notes

Recording Your Visit to the
Overmountain Victory National Historic Trail

(Add the dates you visit each site)

Map Panel # 1 – Abingdon to Choate's Ford

Campbell's Grave   _____

Muster Grounds and surrounding markers   _____

Pemberton Oak   _____

Choate's Ford waysides and markers   _____

Womack's Old Fort marker   _____

      Side trip to Bristol for Isaac Shelby and Fort Shelby markers   _____

Map Panel # 2 – Choate's Ford to Gap Creek

Rocky Mount Museum State Historic Site   _____

      Side trip to Robert Young Cabin   _____

      Side trip to Mary Patton Grave   _____

Sycamore Shoals State Historic Area   _____

      Side trip to Carter Mansion   _____

Gap Creek Monument   _____

Map Panel # 3 – Gap Creek to Roaring Creek

Town of Roan Mountain   _____

Shelving Rock   _____

Shelving Rock Encampment ("The Resting Place")   _____

Hampton Creek Cove State Natural Area   _____

Yellow Mountain Gap   _____

Roaring Creek Road (campsite marker missing)   _____

Map Panel # 4 – Roaring Creek to North Cove and Turkey Cove

Davenport Springs   _____

Robert Sevier Grave   _____

Grassy Creek campsite (marker in Spruce Pine) _____

Gillespie Gap (Museum of North Carolina Minerals)   _____

Hefner Gap/McKinney Gap overlooks   _____

Turkey Cove encampment   _____

North Cove encampment   _____

Map Panel # 5 – North Cove and Turkey Cove to Quaker Meadows

Joseph McDowell House in Marion   _____

Side Trip to Historic Carson House   _____

A GUIDE TO THE OVERMOUNTAIN VICTORY NATIONAL HISTORIC TRAIL

Side Trip to Mountain Gateway Museum _____

Quaker Meadows in Morganton
    Charles McDowell House _____

    Council Oak marker _____

    Quaker Meadows Cemetery _____

    OVNHT along the Catawba River Greenway _____

Map Panel #6 – Elkin Creek to Fort Defiance

Mustering Grounds _____

Benjamin Cleveland marker _____

Wilkes Heritage Museum _____

Tory Oak _____

Robert Cleveland Log Cabin _____

Yadkin River Greenway and OVNHT _____

Moravian Creek Access to Yadkin River Greenway _____

W. Kerr Scott Reservoir Visitor Assistance Center _____

Mountain View Overlook _____

    Side trip to Whippoorwill Academy and Village _____

Fort Defiance _____

Map Panel # 7 – Fort Defiance to Quaker Meadows

Yadkin River Greenway of Caldwell County   _____

Fort Crider site _____

Johns River Crossing   _____

Rocky Ford Access to Catawba River Greenway   _____

Catawba Meadows Park Access to Catawba River Greenway   _____

Map Panel #8 – Quaker Meadows to Gilbert Town

Greenlee Ford Access to Catawba River Greenway   _____

Pilot Mountain _____

Bedford Hill   _____

Cane Creek historical marker   _____

Marlin's Knob   _____

Brittain Church and Cemetery   _____

Gilbert Town marker   _____

Side trip to Rutherford County Office Building   _____

Biggerstaff's Old Fields   _____

Map Panel #9 - Gilbert Town to The Cowpens

Alexander's Ford and Bradley Nature Preserve
(as of spring 2011, not yet open to the public)   _____

Cowpens National Battlefield   _____

Map Panel # 10 – The Cowpens to King's Mountain

Colonel James Williams's Grave   _____

Cherokee Ford   _____

Kings Mountain National Military Park   _____

Three Friends on the Frontier

They were rascals. Before they were heroes, three young men, who would later become icons of the Southern Campaign of the American Revolution, were together in their youth reckless, shiftless, carefree lads. For a time on the Virginia frontier in the mid-1700s, these three friends enjoyed times of untroubled, high-spirited living—frolicking, drinking, gambling and paying little heed to making their way in the world. Ben, Tom, and Joe shared the common bond of youthful irresponsibility during their adolescence and early adulthood. Their devil-may-care lives at the time belied the commitment and resolve each would later exhibit to bring about the hard-fought independence of the United States of America.

The celebrated contributions of these three Patriots in support of the cause of Liberty occurred in different theaters of conflict; and, history usually recounts their stories disconnected from each other. However, their heroic efforts and influences did converge in a most unsuspected way. During the summer and fall of 1780, each, in his own way, helped bring about the Battle of Kings Mountain. Thanks to each, that Patriot victory at the hands of militiamen from the backcountry turned the direction of the Revolutionary War. Though they were scamps in their youth together, Ben, Tom, and Joe grew in character and action to become the noted partisans: Colonel Benjamin Cleaveland, General Thomas Sumter, and General Joseph Martin. Their youthful escapades

Book Excerpt from Before They Were Heroes at King's Mountain

aside, the reputations of these patriots remain indelible in American history. Their connections to one another and to the Battle of Kings Mountain are important links to the broader story of America's beginnings as an independent nation.

Spirited Young Lads

Full of themselves and the passions of youth, in the early 1750s, the three friends joined the local militia in Orange County, then the backcountry of settled Virginia. They served together under Colonel Zachariah Burnley at a time when the world was changing around them.[1] In the mid-1750s, the dominance of Great Britain on the frontier of America was called into question. Lt. Colonel George Washington surrendered Fort Necessity in 1754 and marched away, yielding for the moment the upper Ohio Valley to French control. The British attempted a formidable response, but a small party of French militiamen and their northern Indian allies ambushed the British column and defeated what was generally regarded as the best fighting force in the world. British Major General Edward Braddock and his entourage of British Regulars and Provincial Guard were routed in a massacre along the Monongahela River on July 9, 1755. It is remembered today as Braddock's Defeat.

After this shocking insult to the British army, the three young Virginians joined the colonial troops for a time and served during the French and Indian War.[2] Joseph Martin, born in 1740, and Thomas Sumter, six years Martin's senior, served together under Col. William Bird. They joined in General John Forbes's 1758 campaign that captured Fort Duquesne, the French fort Braddock had failed to conquer. That captured, strategic stronghold was renamed Fort Pitt. By the end of the conflict, Sumter, the oldest of the three, earned his stripes as a sergeant at age 24. The particulars of service during the war of the third lad,

Benjamin Cleaveland, born in 1738, are lost to history but may have included service under Colonel James "Mad Jimmie" Moore.[3]

During the years following the French and Indian War, life drew the three young men in different directions, yet they also shared similar and important molding experiences. Each was a frontiersman, making his way on the edge of a growing America in a time of revolutionary change. The three friends all served separately as leaders of the back-country militia. They faced down Cherokee and Shawnee resistance to expanding white settlement. They all mined their frontier experiences and honed their skills to become men of ability during the two decades before the American Revolution.

Bad Blood Between Allies

The challenges faced by Martin, Sumter, and Cleaveland were rooted in the Colonial period and the betrayal of respect between allies. During the French and Indian War, the Cherokees served as allies of the British. The "Real People" fought alongside the red-coated British Regulars and the uniformed Provincial Guard of the colonies in their fight against the French army and militia and their Indian allies from the north. But, eventually the Cherokees fell from alliance with the British colonists.

Despite making numerous promises, British military leaders mistreated and undersupplied the Cherokees during the first years of the war. In 1758, Cherokee warriors supported Forbes's campaign against Fort Duquesne, but suffered some unstated offense from the British. Cherokee chief Attakullakulla (called Little Carpenter) and nine warriors departed the campaign, but were overtaken at Forbes's instructions and disarmed. The Cherokee braves continued on, bound for home. Before

Three Friends on the Frontier

the chief reached his village, another party of Cherokees also departed the campaign unescorted. These allied warriors had not been compensated properly, and during their trip homeward, they felt obliged to take as payment goods and property from any whites they happened upon. They viewed all English as members of the same tribe, each responsible for a common debt. One group of Virginia militiamen, suffering the loss of their horses to the disgruntled Cherokee warriors, felt differently about the matter. They organized themselves and rode down the Cherokees, killing and scalping a dozen or more as horse thieves.[4] When the survivors reached the Cherokee Nation with the story of these murders at the hands of the English, the young Cherokee warriors were outraged. Taking up arms, they set upon white settlements all along the frontier in the Carolinas and Virginia determined to exact revenge in small and swift attacks. In February 1760, a party of Cherokees killed 50 settlers in the Long Canes of South Carolina as the settlers were attempting to make their way to safety in Augusta.[5] In the same month, another party attacked the British garrison at Fort Dobbs on the North Carolina frontier. The Provincial Guard at the fort repelled the attackers, but the Cherokees massacred settlers living nearby. In the face of this uprising, called the Cherokee War, over half of the white settlers retreated from the North Carolina piedmont frontier. Notable among them, Daniel Boone removed his wife Rebecca and their two sons, James and Israel, from the Forks of the Yadkin to a safe community. His family remained in Culpeper County, Virginia for the duration of the conflict, while he returned to the North Carolina mountains for hunting and perhaps service during the war. (See *In the Footsteps of Daniel Boone*.)

Over the next two years, British units under the successive commands of Colonel Archibald Montgomery and Colonel James Grant along with South Carolina militiamen and volunteers eventually subdued the

Cherokees. In two separate campaigns, the 77th Regiment of Foot and the Highlanders marched into the Cherokee Nation, destroying villages and crops. They attacked the Lower Towns and the Middle Towns. In the second campaign, the British killed 60 to 80 Cherokees, taking another 40 as prisoners, mostly women and children. The soldiers did not intend to fight the Cherokees as much as force them into the mountains to die of starvation and exposure. Among those officers marauding through the Cherokees' Lower and Middle Towns and learning the skills of fighting in the backcountry were Andrew Williamson, Andrew Pickens, Francis Marion, William Moultrie, Henry Laurens, and Isaac Huger. All these men would play important roles later during the Southern Campaign of the American Revolution.[6]

Despairing of the destruction of his homeland, Cherokee leader Attakullakulla helped negotiate a peace in both Charlestown, South Carolina and at Fort Robinson, recently built on the Long Island of the Holston River (in today's Kingsport, Tennessee). Speaking for Chief Kanagatucko (called Standing Turkey), Attakullakulla told the Royal governor and the military officers at the two separate treaties that the Cherokee chiefs were sorry they had started a war. When he signed a peace treaty on November 19, 1761 at Fort Robinson, then under the command of Colonel Adam Stephen, Kanagatucko asked that one of the Virginia soldiers carry the treaty to the Overhill Towns to demonstrate the good intentions of the British. Sensing the personal danger this arrangement would create for any courier should the British violate the treaty, Stephen was reluctant to order any of his men to go. Not willing to see the peace pact undone, Lieutenant Henry Timberlake volunteered for the mission. Demonstrating no less courage in the face of such danger, Sergeant Thomas Sumter volunteered to go with him.

Three Friends on the Frontier

Book Excerpt from Before They Were Heroes at King's Mountain

Thomas Sumter

Though the Cherokees warned Timberlake and Sumter that travel by water would expose them to the hostilities of French-allied northern Indians along the way, the small party departed by canoe on November 28. They expected to arrive in the Overhill Towns by descending the Holston and Cherokee rivers in six days.[7] Joined by an interpreter, John McCormack, the party took with them in a large canoe supplies for ten days and goods enough to trade for horses for their return trip. To outfit this expedition, Sumter borrowed £60 from Alexander McDonald.

Not far below the Long Island, the men ran aground in shallow water. Timberlake recorded, "Sumter the serjeant leaped out, and dragged us near a hundred yards over the shoals until we found deep water again."[8] Suffering the effects of the summer's drought, the river's shallow water plagued the men for the next 19 days as winter quickly approached. They spent much of each day dragging the canoe and supplies. Timberlake recalled, ". . . the weather was so extremely cold, that the ice hung to our cloaths . . ."[9]

With provisions running low, one of the party went ashore to hunt, but one of their two guns broke in firing. From the canoe, Sumter attempted to steady himself for a shot at a bear, but succeeded only in knocking the remaining good rifle overboard, losing it in a deep pool. Their circumstances were dire. "Our provisions were consumed to an ounce of meat and but very little flour," Timberlake wrote, "our guns lost and spoiled, ourselves in the heart of woods, at a season when neither fruit nor roots were to be found, many days journey from any habitation and frequented only by the northern Indians from whom we had more reason to expect scalping than succor."[10] Remarkably, the men succeeded in some unreliable, makeshift manner to repair the broken rifle sufficiently—and with much good luck—to kill a bear. They would not starve, it seemed.

Proceeding down river, they encountered an "amazing quantity of buffaloes, bears, deer, beavers, geese, swans, ducks, turkeys and other game,"[11] Timberlake recounted. They stopped to explore a cave high on a bluff along the river. For lack of light they could not venture far in; and, upon their quick return to the river, they discovered their canoe drifting away. Sumter scampered down the near-vertical face of the bluff, jumped into the river without even removing his coat and swam after the canoe. He caught it a quarter-mile downstream. With Sumter's clothes soaked and frozen stiff, the men built a fire in the cave to dry him out. The three did not sleep much at all that night because of the continual wailing of wild beasts trapped farther back in the cave by the men's campfire at its mouth. When they did depart after two nights, they discovered a substantial waterfall not far below the spot where Sumter had stopped the canoe. Had he not recovered it when he did, they would certainly have lost all their trade goods, their gear, and the renewed supply of meat.

During the next few days, the explorers negotiated their way downriver past massive, stair-stepped waterfalls and broke a path through long expanses of bank-to-bank ice. At the end of that ordeal, a Cherokee hunting party intercepted the adventurers. Taking some pity on the hapless travelers, this band of Cherokees led the expedition downriver and then upstream against the current along a wide tributary to the Overhill Towns. During the following two months, Timberlake and Sumter lived among the Cherokees visiting Tommotley, Chote, Settico, Chilhowee, and other villages along the river. Timberlake kept a detailed diary and sketched a map of the Cherokee towns throughout the region. He

Three Friends on the Frontier

Book Excerpt from Before They Were Heroes at King's Mountain

named the river for the town of Tanasi and recorded it on his map the way he heard it, "Tennessee." During this time of exploration, Sumter and Timberlake continued developing their skills with the Cherokee language.

On March 10, 1762, Timberlake, Sumter, and the interpreter departed Tommotley and headed back to Fort Robinson, escorted by Chief Ostenaco (also called Judd's Friend or Judge[12]) and some one hundred Cherokee braves and village chieftains. Concluding his visit at the fort, Ostenaco asked if they might go to Williamsburg where he hoped to see the governor. Accommodating the request, Sumter and Timberlake escorted a party of Cherokee chiefs to the Virginia capital where the governor entertained the visiting Cherokee for several weeks. At a departure dinner held at the College of William and Mary, Ostenaco saw a portrait of King George III,[13] and he expressed a desire to meet "the King my father." Initially reluctant to arrange the trip, Lieutenant Governor Francis Fauquier eventually chose to send Ostenaco and two other chiefs, Cunne Shote (called Stalking Turkey) and Wooe (alsoWoyi, called Pidgeon), to London.[14] Timberlake and Sumter accompanied the chiefs along with a new interpreter. Thomas Jefferson, then a student at the college, later recalled hearing Ostenaco bid his people farewell the night before the departure: "The moon was in full splendour, and to her he seemed to address himself in his prayers for his own safety on the voyage and that of his people during his absence. His sounding voice, distinct articulation, animated action, and the solemn silence of his people at their several fires, filled me with awe and veneration, although I did not understand a word he uttered."[15]

On June 16, the Cherokee chiefs and their colonial escorts arrived at Plymouth, England and later London to great curiosity. London society

BEFORE THEY WERE HEROES AT KING'S MOUNTAIN

Cherokee Chief Ostenaco, joined by Cunne Shote and Wooe and escorted by Henry Timberlake and Thomas Sumter, traveled to London to meet with King George III in 1762. The Museum of the Cherokee Indian in Cherokee, NC presents this tableau as part of its "Emissaries of Peace" exhibit, interpreting the 1762 Cherokee and British delegations.

and aristocracy so grandly received the chiefs that Timberlake and Sumter purchased scarlet coats for their uniforms and passed themselves off as British officers. After weeks of various receptions, tours, and portrait sessions, the chiefs enjoyed an audience with King George III, then just 24 years of age and in his second year on the throne. Because the skilled interpreter had died on the voyage over, Sumter and Timberlake stepped in and served as best they could at translating the exchange between his Majesty and the three Cherokees.[16] The parties each offered gifts and pledges of loyalty and friendship. Departing Great Britain, the Cherokees sailed to Charlestown with Sumter escorting them; Timberlake remained behind. The travelers arrived October 28. At the chief's insistence, Sumter rode with them through the South Carolina countryside and stayed for a while longer in the Overhill

Three Friends on the Frontier

Book Excerpt from Before They Were Heroes at King's Mountain

Thomas Sumter opened a store in South Carolina in 1767 after escaping from a jail in Virginia. A badly weathered historical marker along SC Hwy 6 in northwest Berkeley County commemorates his "country store." (See Notes for marker text.)

Towns. During the ride, Sumter admired the landscape they passed. During his second stay, he earned the Cherokees' deeper friendship. In the spring, Sumter departed the Cherokee villages and returned to Virginia by way of Charlestown, again delighting in the South Carolina backcountry on his journey.

Arriving home in Virginia among friends and family in early 1763, Thomas Sumter was welcomed warmly. He recounted his exploits and experiences of the recent several years to an eager audience of neighbors. Alexander McDonald was glad to see him as well, but for another reason. Sumter had not repaid the £60 he had borrowed for the expedition into the Cherokee Nation more than a year before. For that reason, McDonald swore out a warrant. After the court convened in November, Thomas Sumter was thrown into jail for debt and held in a gaol in Staunton. Good fortune and a good friend, however, soon rescued the adventurer. Joseph Martin was returning home from his service in the military when he arrived in Staunton. Learning of Sumter's

BEFORE THEY WERE HEROES AT KING'S MOUNTAIN

plight, Martin went to visit his old childhood friend. After gaining permission to spend the night at the gaol so he could talk to his friend, Martin departed in the morning, having left Sumter a tomahawk and 10 guineas (pounds sterling). By use of one or both, Sumter escaped the jail the next day and headed south. Arriving safely in South Carolina, the fugitive wrote to Joseph Martin three weeks later from Long Cane Creek, declaring " . . . I am for Ever your Honest Friend."[17]

Shortly thereafter, Thomas Sumter ventured to the land he had spied in passing through South Carolina. He established a store not far off the Santee River, where roads converged, connecting the coastal region with the Upcountry. He prospered quickly and invested his profits in more land. In the summer of 1767, Sumter married; and, he married well. Taking as his wife the widow Mary Jameson, Sumter gained a sizeable plantation at the Great Savannah at Nelson's Ferry across the Santee River.[18] As a prominent member of the community, Sumter and his associates were friends of the government and supporters of the King and Parliament. But, when the revolution came and after hearing the arguments for independence from Great Britain offered by young firebrands in the community, Sumter soon changed his Loyalist attitude and became an ardent supporter of Liberty. [19]

Joseph Martin

In his youth, Joseph Martin was regarded as "large, rude, and ungovernable."[20] His unwillingness to attend to his education caused his father to hire him out as an apprentice carpenter. He rebelled against the instruction, ran away, and joined the provincial guard at Fort Pitt with his friends. Returning home after his service, Martin came into a small inheritance from his father who had died in 1760. Though married in 1762, Martin refused to reform his wild ways. He never drank to excess,

Three Friends on the Frontier

Book Excerpt from Before They Were Heroes at King's Mountain

nor was he given to swearing profanely, but he enjoyed gambling, perhaps too much. Soon enough Martin found his inheritance gone and himself in debt.

Martin was adventurous and resourceful enough, however, to work his way out of financial trouble. He became a long hunter and may well have ventured into southwest Virginia in the early 1760s with Elijah Wallen. (It is said Wallen was the first to have applied the name "Cumberland" from the river, named by Dr. Thomas Walker in 1748, to the prominent pass then known as Cave Gap.) But aside from the hard work of the long hunt, Martin also fancied to find easy ways he might make his living without much toil. Joining him in the effort to shirk such enterprising industry as drudgery was his childhood friend, Benjamin Cleaveland, another notably idle and married roustabout who also favored riotous living.

Cleaveland and Martin were good hunters and certainly much preferred to go on long hunts than to work on their family farms. Martin's "restless spirit could not be patient at the plow," his son later recounted.[21] The pair ranged far and wide through south central Virginia collecting hides, pelts, and furs from the headwaters of the Staunton (Roanoke), Pigg, and Dan rivers. They had a good market for the skins they harvested. By such efforts over several years and by some good success in his continued gambling, Martin worked himself out of debt. He also earned a deserved reputation as a more-than-competent backwoodsman.

In 1767 while still looking for easy ways to make a living, Cleaveland and Martin attempted to plant a crop of wheat on Cleaveland's land along the Pigg River. The young men were rather lazy about tending the crop, however, and did not properly fence it to protect it from wild

BEFORE THEY WERE HEROES AT KING'S MOUNTAIN

animals. At harvest time, as was the custom—and certainly their preference—they invited some friends to help with cutting what wheat there was. To ease the anticipated drudgery on the eve of beginning work, Cleaveland and Martin offered the gathering adequate liquor and the inspirations of a fiddler. The group enjoyed a spirited evening of revelry but never did get around to harvesting any grain. The crop and the enterprise were lost.[22]

Two years later, Martin took up a challenge offered by Dr. Thomas Walker to settle land Walker claimed in the Powell River valley (today's Lee County, Virginia). Walker offered two teams of adventurers—Martin's party and the Kirtleys—the challenge to venture west and put in a crop of corn in the prize region. The first group there would win claims on extensive tracts of fertile land. Martin's group stood to gain 21,000 acres of their choosing.

Following a four-day trip from home to Staunton, Martin's group arrived at the New River on March 14, 1769. There at Captain English's fort, they provisioned their party with seed corn and ammunition. When they reached the Holston River, they learned that Captain [Angus?] Rucker[23] and the Kirtleys had days before hired a pilot to take them by the quickest route to the Powell River valley. Martin's party was already behind, they realized. They hired their own pilot and hurried into the fray with an advance party; the remaining party would follow. After three days, the advance team was lost, and spent another three days wandering around looking for a path. They crossed mountains, creeks, laurel, and canebrakes.[24] The land was rugged. The men were hungry and the horses exhausted. They rested another two days, when Martin, exploring some five miles from the camp, came upon the Hunter's Track. He hurried back to camp with the good news. The men departed the next morning on the 24th with renewed hope and no small

Three Friends on the Frontier

Book Excerpt from Before They Were Heroes at King's Mountain

In 1769, Joseph Martin and his men built a fortified station along Beargrass Creek on the far western Virginia frontier, but it was soon destroyed by Cherokee or Shawnee raiders. Wilderness Road State Park in Lee County, Virginia interprets Martin's Station and hosts juried reenactments.

portion of anger. "With much difficulty," Martin wrote, "I prevented my companions from discharging our pilot with heavy blows." The advance party arrived at the Powell Valley two days later and the remainder of the men arrived on April 1.[25] In short order they began to secure their sustenance from the forest, consuming in six weeks "23 deer— 15 bears—2 buffaloes and a great number of turkeys." On the 15th, the Kirtleys arrived, but discovering they had been beat to the site, they turned homeward without looking elsewhere for claims.

Martin was delighted with the land. He described it as possessing "Vast quantities of black Walnut and wild cherries . . .Very good Springs— Bold creeks, big enough for Mills."[26] Word of this rich land had already attracted others. He wrote, "April 24th came several gentlemen from Culpeper, with negroes to Settle. Likewise several gentleman from Bed-

BEFORE THEY WERE HEROES AT KING'S MOUNTAIN

ford, 3 gentlemen from Maryland, to get land to settle 100 families." And while Joseph Martin and his men were busily constructing Martin's Station along Beargrass Creek, Daniel Boone and his party of five other hunters were surprised to happen upon any white settlement that far into the wilderness. Boone had left his home on the Upper Yadkin River on May 1 upon the hope that John Finley did indeed know how to find a passage through the Cumberland Mountains, one that would take them into the abundant hunting lands of Ken-te-ke. (See *In the Footsteps of Daniel Boone.*)

Martin's men erected the frontier station and put in a crop of corn. They too ventured into Ken-te-ke to hunt. A party of Indians—probably Cherokee or Shawnee—befriended the party of hunters long enough to gain their trust. After a time and on a signal, the Indians seized all the inattentive hunters' rifles. The captors sent the men back east through the gap. When the would-be hunters reached the station, they discovered it had been broken up. Despairing of the Indian menace for the time being, Martin and his men abandoned the station and returned home. Martin spent the next three years working as an overseer on a relative's plantation. He saved his earnings and purchased his own tract for farming in Pittsylvania County (later Henry County), Virginia. He moved there in 1773.

Benjamin Cleaveland

The seriousness of enterprise that would later mark the life of Benjamin Cleaveland continued to escape the young man who was idly enjoying an undirected life. About 1764 and after serving in some manner during the French and Indian War, he married Mary Graves of Orange County, Virginia. Her father was well-to-do and so there was little pressure for Cleaveland to embark in earnest on his own endeavor. He continued to enjoy horse-racing and gambling. Without apology, he

Three Friends on the Frontier

engaged with his circle of rowdy friends, including Joseph Martin, in the frolicking that was customary on the frontier.

Except for the impending (or possibly recent) birth of Cleaveland's third child in 1769, Cleaveland would likely have gone with Joseph Martin on his expedition to the Powell River valley. Or it may be that Cleaveland's father-in-law was too insistent on separating the young man from his frolicking friends. In either case, Benjamin Cleaveland and family departed for the backcountry of North Carolina when that third child was but an infant.

Near 1770, the young Cleaveland family, along with his father-in-law, Mr. Graves, settled in the foothills of the Blue Ridge Mountains along Roaring River, a tributary of the Yadkin River. With labor provided by the workers enslaved by Mr. Graves, a Cleaveland farmstead began raising crops and livestock. Meanwhile, Benjamin Cleaveland continued to hunt. At some point, he scouted far enough to the southeast to find a site where he erected a new home for his family. It lay in a horseshoe bend of the Yadkin River, about three miles downstream from the mouth of Roaring River. There he built his home which he named "The Round About." During 1770, Surry County was formed from Rowan County and Benjamin Cleaveland became one of its prominent leaders, serving as a justice of the court.

After completing his initial two-year long hunt into Ken-te-ke, Daniel Boone returned home to the Upper Yadkin Valley in the spring of 1771 not too far from the home of Benjamin Cleaveland. Boone's brother, Squire, Jr., had returned during the interim on several occasions with deer hides and peltry to sell. He also brought with him stories of the success of their hunts and he told of the herds of buffalo and the forests abundantly rife with deer, elk, otter and beaver. With these sto-

BEFORE THEY WERE HEROES AT KING'S MOUNTAIN

ries circulating in the communities of the Yadkin River valley and perhaps after hearing them directly from Daniel Boone himself, Cleaveland decided a hunting expedition would be his next adventure.

In the summer of 1772, Cleaveland, in the company of Jesse Walton, Jesse Bond, Edward Rice, and William Hightower, made his way into Ken-te-ke.[27] The route to Cumberland Gap was known to adventurous hunters. In the Powell Valley, he no doubt passed by the settlement his good friend Joseph Martin had built three years earlier and then shortly abandoned in the face of Indian attacks. After crossing through the Gap, Cleaveland's party was itself set upon by a band of Cherokees. The braves threatened the hunters and then took all their possessions including not only the hides and pelts they had collected, but their horses, guns, powder, and shot. The irate Cherokees also took the trespassers' hats and shoes as well. They warned the explorers never to come back to their hunting grounds and then gave the men an old shotgun and enough powder and shot for just two loads. Cleaveland's party retreated toward North Carolina taking care to save their powder for a sure kill. They did shoot one small deer, but missed the intended mark with the other shot. With luck, they caught a wild

After living on Roaring River for a few years, Benjamin Cleaveland moved his family to a site in a bend of the Yadkin River. He named the home he built there "The Round About." A marker along NC Hwy 268 near Ronda commemorates his home.

Three Friends on the Frontier

Book Excerpt from Before They Were Heroes at King's Mountain

goose suffering with a broken wing. This provided the only other food they had. Nearing starvation, Cleaveland killed his faithful hunting dog to feed himself and his friends. In later years and speaking kindly of this four-legged hunting companion, Cleaveland said it was the "sweetest animal food" he had ever eaten. Supplementing this meager fare with only wild berries and nuts, Cleaveland and his party eventually arrived home, but they were severely undernourished. They had nearly starved to death.

After regaining his strength over the following few months, Cleaveland declared he would recover the horses that had been stolen from him. Hightower, at least, was among the band of hand-picked men who accompanied Cleaveland into Cherokee territory. They arrived first at Nikwasi (Neequasee),[28] the village of the Cherokee chief Yona Equa (called Big Bear).[29] He told Cleaveland that the horses were in the Cherokee towns farther west and that the warriors who had them would likely kill Cleaveland and his party when they arrived. As a compliment, Yona Equa added, "If you were to be killed, I should claim that honor, as one big warrior ought only be slain by another."[30] Cleaveland was indeed uncommonly big and strong, weighing well over 300 pounds even in the prime of life. He boasted that his muscular power was limited only by the strength of his bones.[31] He was a good-natured man, but at times, he could be hot tempered; most definitely he was determined. To help Cleaveland in recovering his stolen property, Yona Equa sent Cherokee escorts along with the hunters.

Cleaveland's party and escorts ventured deeper into the Cherokee Nation and soon without much trouble had reclaimed all the horses except his. When the party rode into the last village, the Cherokee brave who had Cleaveland's horse raised his tomahawk in a threat. Cleaveland cocked his rifle and pointed it toward the man. One of the escorts threw himself against the brave knocking him to the ground to keep him from being shot. The indignant Cherokee, however, had already thrown his tomahawk. It reached its mark, but only cut away part of Cleaveland's hunting shirt.

Cleaveland mounted his recovered horse and was riding away when the angry brave shot Cleaveland's horse. The injury was not serious and Cleaveland rode on. The party of hunters returned to Yona Equa who, perhaps, was impressed that all the horses had actually been recovered. He increased the number of escorts to see the men safely out of the Cherokee Nation. On their return home, Cleaveland's party rode through the Tugaloo area giving Cleaveland his first look at the picturesque and bountiful land where he would later live.

A New Time Coming

In the mid-1770s, tensions between the American colonies and the British Ministers continued to mount as Great Britain sought ways to pay off the heavy debt of having fought the Seven Years' War. Revolution was in the air. The backcountry regions of North Carolina and Virginia, however, were not as preoccupied with revolutionary talk as were the eastern counties, although neighbors and relations were soon to choose sides, just as they would in the backcountry of South Carolina and Georgia. Events soon to unfold would once again test the mettle of the three childhood friends from Virginia's Orange County. This would not be a time for childishness. This was a time for heroes.

Three Friends on the Frontier

Book Excerpt from Before They Were Heroes at King's Mountain

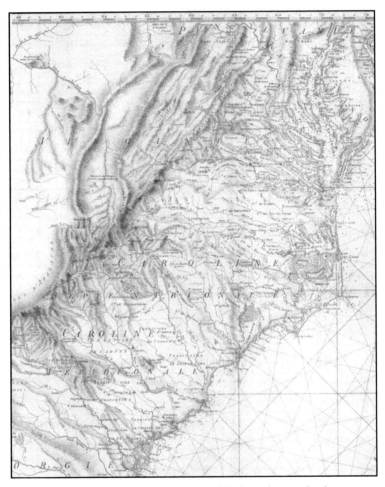

**Detail from a map of the British American colonies
by French cartographer, Antoine de Sartine, 1778**

The four maps on the following pages show the sites of events shared in *Before They Were Heroes at King's Mountain*. All editions include the story of the muster, march, and pursuit by the Patriots and the battle at King's Mountain. The additional sites covered in the full edition and each regional edition are as shown.

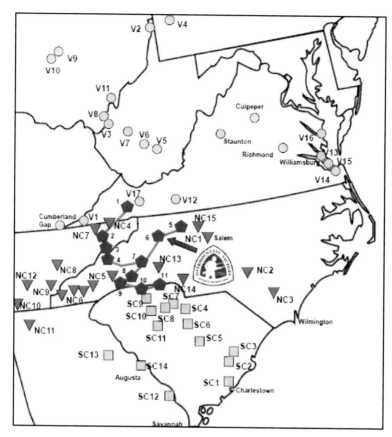

This map shows the locations of key sites for events from 1774 to 1780. Many additional nearby sites are mentioned in the accounts. This map shows current state outlines of the Southern region to help orient readers to the places mentioned in the accounts.

Numbered sites for the Overmountain Victory National Historic Trail are:

1 - Abingdon Muster Grounds

2 - Sycamore Shoals

3 - Yellow Mountain Gap

4 - Gillespie Gap

5 - Surry Mustering Grounds

6 - Tory Oak and The Round About

7 - Quaker Meadows

8 - Gilbert Town

9 - Green River ford (Alexander's)

10 - The Cowpens

11 - Little King's Mountian

Book Excerpt from Before They Were Heroes at King's Mountain

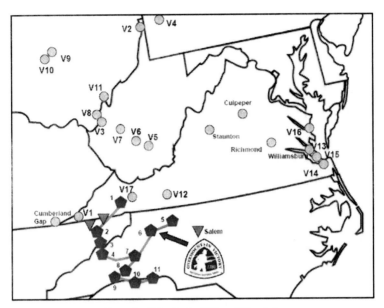

**Sites in Virginia, West Virginia,
Pennsylvania, and Ohio**

V1 -- Martin's Station, Wilderness Road State Park

V2 – Yellow Creek Massacre

V3 -- George Washington's Land Grant

V4 – Fort Dunmore (site of Fort Pitt)

V5 – Camp Union (today's Lewisburg, WV)

V6 -- Grandview State Park

V7 – Kanawha River at Elk River (today's Charleston, WV)

V8 – Battle of Point Pleasant (Tu-Endie-Wei State Park)

V9 – Camp Charlotte

V10 – Logan Elm State Memorial

V11 – Fort Gower

V12 – Lead Mines

V13 – Williamsburg

V14 – Battle of Great Bridge

V15 – Bombardment of Norfolk

V16 – Gwynn's Island

V17 – Aspenvale

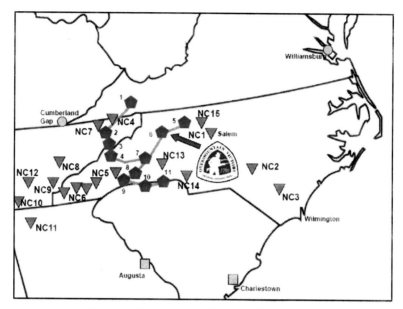

Sites in North Carolina and Tennessee

NC1 – Salem
NC2 – Cross Creek (Fayetteville)
NC3 – Moores Creek National Battlefield
NC4 – Overmountain Region (Holston, Watauga, and
        Nolichucky river valleys)
NC5 – Fort Davidson (Old Fort)
NC6 – Middle Towns of Cherokee (Rutherford's Campaign)
NC7 – Long Island of the Holston (Kingsport)
NC8 – Warrior's Path, French Broad River
NC9 – Towns of the Overhill Cherokee
NC10 – Chickamauga Creek (Chattanooga)
NC11 – Chickamauga refuge
NC12 – Sale Creek
NC13 – Battle of Ramsour's Mill
NC14 – Battle of Charlotte
NC15 – Bethabara and Bethania

Book Excerpt from Before They Were Heroes at King's Mountain

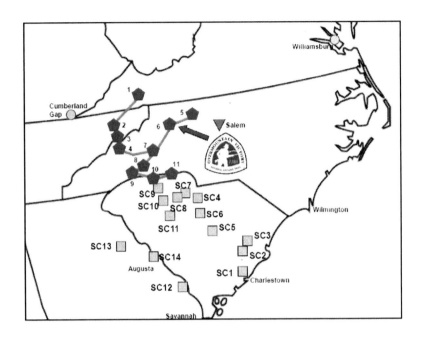

Sites in South Carolina and Georgia

SC1 – Charlestown

SC2 – Biggin's Bridge (Monck's Corner)

SC3 – Lenud's Ferry

SC4 – Waxhaws (Buford's Massacre)

SC5 – High Hills of Santee (Thomas Sumter's home)

SC6 –Camden

SC7 – Rocky Mount

SC8 – Hanging Rock

SC9 – Thicketty Fort

SC10 –Musgrove's Mill

SC11 – Ninety Six

SC12 – Battle of Briar Creek

SC13 – Battle of Kettle Creek

SC14 – Siege of Augusta

Before They Were Heroes at King's Mountain
is available from the publisher,
Daniel Boone Footsteps

Write to:
Daniel Boone Footsteps
1959 N. Peace Haven Rd., # 105
Winston-Salem, NC 27106

DBooneFootsteps@gmail.com

Purchase online at:
www.danielboonefootsteps.com

or support one of the Eastern National bookstores
at National Park sites along the
Overmountain Victory National Historic Trail.

Book Excerpt from Before They Were Heroes at King's Mountain

CPSIA information can be obtained at www.ICGtesting.com
Printed in the USA
LVOW111529120513

333384LV00011B/270/P

9 780976 914952